SUBMARINES

Explore underwater vessels from the early days to the present

PaRragon

Bath·New York·Singapore·Hong Kong·Cologne·Delhi·Melbourne

First published by Parragon in 2010
Parragon
Queen Street House
4 Queen Street
Bath BA1 1HE, UK

Copyright © Parragon Books Ltd 2010

ISBN: 978-1-4075-5568-3

Editorial and design by
Amber Books Ltd
Bradley's Close
74–77 White Lion Street
London N1 9PF
United Kingdom
www.amberbooks.co.uk

Project Editor: Sarah Uttridge
Design: Rick Fawcett
Picture Research: Terry Forshaw

Printed in China

PICTURE CREDITS

Cover: Main image: Michael Melford/Getty Images
Bottom left: Royal Navy Submarine Museum
Bottom, second and third from left: Cody images
Bottom right: Getty Images

Amber Books: 11 bottom, 17 right, 68 both, 71, 73 top right
Art-Tech/Aerospace: 8, 35 bottom, 41 bottom, 45 bottom, 48, 49 centre & bottom, 53,
58 bottom, 66 top, 81
Art-Tech/De Agostini: 13 bottom, 24 top, 28 bottom, 54
Art-Tech/MARS: 17 left, 18 bottom, 23 right, 24 bottom, 31 bottom, 36 top, 39 top
Cody Images: 9, 19 both, 20/21, 21, 23 left, 26/27, 28 top, 29, 31 top, 36 bottom, 37, 38/39, 40 top, 41 top,
42/43, 43, 45 top & centre, 46/47, 47, 49 top, 50/51, 51, 57 bottom, 67
Corbis: 32/33 (Bettmann), 63 bottom (EPA/Guang Niu), 77 top (Ralph White)
Getty Images: 27 (Hulton Archive), 34 top (Popperfoto), 34 bottom (Hulton Archive), 40 bottom (Hulton Archive),
44 (Popperfoto), 54/55, 60/61, 63 top (AFP), 70/71 (AFP), 78 (API/Vanderlei Almedia)
National Undersea Research Program: 74-76 all, 79 both
Royal Navy Submarine Museum: 16 both, 18 top, 22/23, 25, 30, 35 top, 39 bottom, 52/53, 73 top left
U.S. Department of Defense: 6/7, 10, 11 top, 12 all, 13 top, 56/57, 57 top, 58 top, 59, 61, 62, 64/65, 65, 66 bottom,
69, 72, 73 bottom, 77 bottom
U.S. National Archives: 14/15

Contents

Introduction

Submarines are used in conflicts throughout the world; they are a vital part of modern-day warfare. This book will examine how they started off as an idea in the sixteenth century to how they have become essential vessels that patrol the seas.

LEFT: USS *Florida* is an *Ohio* class ballistic missile submarine. The *Ohio* class boat is the largest type of submarine ever constructed for the US Navy.

Introduction

The idea of a vessel that could

travel beneath the surface was put forward at various times in history. The concept was not all that far-fetched – parts of a ship were below the waterline, after all. However, there were numerous technical problems to solve before a working submarine could be built.

A submersible vessel obviously needs to be watertight throughout its hull, including any hatches or other openings. It needs to be propelled in some manner, and its direction must be controllable. It must be possible to submerge and rise to the surface again, which requires a form of control not used aboard surface ships. Finally, the crew must be able to breathe while submerged. The only means of power available to early experimenters was human muscle – and mechanical systems were the only way this power could be used. These factors greatly limited what could be achieved. Early submarines used hand-cranked propellers, with the strength and endurance of the crew defining the maximum power to weight ratio of the vessel. The heavy manual labour required to propel a vessel also used up the air inside at an increased rate.

It was the development of the internal combustion engine, along with other inventions such as compressed air, that made the submarine a practicable vessel. An engine provided motive power, but there were other advantages too. Compressed air enabled the crew to breathe for extended periods and helped solve the problem of diving and surfacing. As a result, submersibles were at first little more than an interesting novelty, with few practical applications.

However, the military capabilities of such a vessel were apparent to some forward-looking thinkers, who tried to develop manually-powered submersible attack craft. In later years, peaceful uses were found for submarines. These included underwater exploration and construction, rescue and transportation. Today, tourist submarines are in use all over the world, allowing paying passengers to experience the undersea environment close up.

Key Components

There are several defining factors for a submarine. Speed and underwater endurance are two, but the depth at which the boat can operate is also critical. Most boats are rated for a safe depth (known as test depth) and can survive somewhat deeper before 'crush depth' is reached. Crush depth is the point where water pressure will cause the

ABOVE: 'A' class submarines of the Royal Navy. Most served in the harbour defence role during World War I.

LEFT: Powered by a steam engine, *Resurgam* successfully conducted trials but sank whilst under tow.

boat's structure to fail, imploding the boat and killing the crew. All submarines need certain components, namely a hull, propulsion system, sensors, control mechanisms and the various systems required to support the crew. Mission-specific equipment, such as weapons for a military submarine, are necessary if the boat is to be more than a novelty.

The crew areas and other critical components of a submarine are contained within the 'pressure hull', which is usually in the form of one or more tubes. Some boats have multiple pressure hulls linked at only a few points, but most have a single pressure hull. Those components that do not need to be protected against water pressure are located outside the pressure hull, which saves space within. They may be between the pressure hull and the outer hull, or

attached to the outside of the boat.

There is a difference between a boat with a 'double hull' and one that has more than one pressure hull. The former refers to a boat that has an unpressurised outer casing, within which the pressure hull and outside components rest. A single-hulled vessel has only a single layer of hull metal between the occupants and the waters outside, though the pressure hull may be in several sections which are connected only at a few points. Most modern boats are single-hulled, with 'light' sections of hull covering components that do not need to be pressurised. There is, however, a move back towards double hulls in the hope of gaining improved damage resistance and increased stealth capabilities.

Until the end of World War II, submarines were really just surface craft that could submerge, rather than true undersea vessels. Their hull form reflected this – other than very early experimental craft, most boats were shaped for surface speed and to reduce rolling, rather than being efficiently streamlined for improved underwater

performance. This in turn, affected other characteristics. For example, diving performance is of lesser interest to a boat that spends most of its time underwater, than to one that cruises on the surface and must crash-dive to escape air or surface attack. Therefore, the ability to dive quickly ceased to be a critical feature of submarine design once the ability to remain submerged was achieved.

Depth Control

It has been said, in grim jest, that all ships can submerge, but only submarines can surface. There is much truth in this – controlling the vessel's ability to dive and to return to the surface presented early experimenters with serious challenges. Among the solutions that were attempted was to hang bags of stones on the sides of an experimental submersible boat. This was a rather imprecise method – one experimental boat in the 1770s worked reasonably well and surfaced again when the bolts holding the bags in place were released. A later attempt with a larger boat resulted in the craft vanishing beneath the surface, never to reappear.

A more effective method of depth control was necessary. As early as 1580, the basic concepts of displacement and buoyancy were understood by some inventors. These ideas were applied in various ways. Some experimental submariners tried to create a boat whose displacement could be altered, simply by sliding sections of the hull in and out. The idea emerged that by fitting compartments into a hull which could be flooded, it was possible to ballast the boat to the point where it would sink, or to pump air into the ballast tanks so that the water was displaced. Early experimenters tried to use collapsible compartments or watertight bags, squeezing water out rather than pumping air in. This was mainly due to the limitations of the available technology and was not effective, though it represented a move in the right direction.

Displacing water with air effectively lightened the boat and caused it to rise to the surface. By carefully controlling the amount of water and air in the tanks it was possible to create 'neutral buoyancy'. In this state, the vessel would remain at its current depth. Additional control was provided by hydroplanes, which could be angled up and down. Just as the vessel's rudder caused it to turn, the hydroplanes angled the boat up or down and allowed fine control of its depth. However, a boat had to be moving reasonably quickly before hydroplanes had any effect, and that, in turn, required solving the propulsion problem.

Propulsion Systems

Hand-powered submersibles proved to have rather limited capabilities whatever means of final drive was employed. There were really two options – oars or screws. Attempts to build oar-powered submarine boats were not effective despite some clever innovations such as self-feathering oars. On a conventional boat, it was normal to lift the oars out of the water when returning to position for another stroke. This is impossible on an underwater boat, potentially resulting in the ludicrous situation where a submersible simply moved back and forth in place as the oarsmen struggled. This problem was solved by creating oars that turned themselves sideways to reduce drag on the forward stroke. Although clever, this did not solve the fundamental problems with oar power.

A screw, or propeller, was a much better option. A screw could be driven by one or more men turning handles or operating pedals, and in some cases was powered by crewmembers walking in treadmills. Screws were found to be an effective means of underwater propulsion and remained in use once engines to power them became available. Various forms of engine were tried. Steam plants never really worked in submarines, although it could be argued that a nuclear boat which uses a reactor to power a steam turbine is a steam-powered submarine; at least of a sort. Traditional furnace-powered steam plants often made the boat too hot for the crew, and attempts to use steam power on the surface and 'residual steam' for underwater movement were not successful.

In the end it was the internal combustion engine, driven by petrol or diesel, which powered most early submarines. Instead of driving the

LEFT: High-quality construction is vital to a submarine. Any weak point can cause the hull to fail, dooming the vessel.

propeller shafts directly from the engines, it was found to be more effective to use an electric motor to drive the shafts. This in turn, was powered from batteries charged by the diesel motor. The chief advantages to this arose from the fact that the boat could run on battery power when submerged, which was not only quieter but also used up less air.

Schnorkel Invention

This diesel-electric system meant that early submarines were much slower underwater than they were on the surface, and tended to operate as surface craft that could submerge when needed, rather than true submarines. The invention of the schnorkel, which allowed the submarine to take in air while keeping the hull submerged, was an important step forward. However, the problem of needing air for the engines was not really solved until the advent of nuclear power. A nuclear boat can remain underwater for months at a time, using recycling systems to clean the air inside for the crew to breathe.

Nuclear power is not acceptable to all nations, and in recent years new technologies have appeared which parallel the capabilities of a nuclear boat while using more conventional power. These are grouped under the heading of AIP (Air-Independent Propulsion) systems.

An attempt at an AIP system was made during World War II, using hydrogen peroxide to provide oxygen to run a diesel engine. Hydrogen peroxide is an extremely dangerous material however, and while this system worked, it was very prone to accidents.

A rather more useful system is to run a conventional diesel engine using a mix of liquid oxygen and the engine's own exhaust gases. This is known as a closed-cycle engine and is not truly air-independent as it needs oxygen, but it is stored aboard rather than needing to be brought in from the outside environment. Liquid oxygen is stored in a 'torus', comprising a tube wound vertically around the pressure hull. There are other possible variations on this theme, but most require the boat to

LEFT: The Swedish *Gotland* class were the first submarines in the world to employ an Air-Independent Propulsion (AIP) system.

BELOW: Buoyancy is controlled by flooding compartments in the outer hull, or by forcing water out using compressed air.

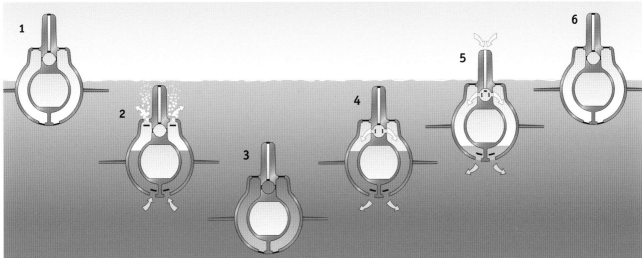

1 The vessel at full buoyancy, sitting on a cushion of air in the ballast tanks.
2 Main vents open; air rushes out, water rushes in destroying positive buoyancy.
3 The submarine sinks and achieves neutral buoyancy. Main vents are shut.

4 High-pressure air is blown into the ballast tanks and expels the water.
5 The submarine, now lighter (less dense), begins to rise.
6 The submarine is back on the surface, fully buoyant.

carry a store of liquid oxygen for use as an oxidant. The effect is the same in all cases – to greatly extend underwater endurance.

Sensors

Some submarines have glazed windows to see out of, usually accompanied by powerful lights, but the sensor system of choice is SONAR. SONAR relies on the propagation of sound waves through water to build up a picture of what is ahead of, around and underneath the submarine.

When it was first invented, SONAR was given the name ASDIC by the British. There are various suggestions as to what this acronym stood for. The most likely is that it arose as a contraction of the code names given to some components to preserve secrecy, though it was later claimed that it came from Allied Submarine Detection Investigation Committee, an organization that itself appears to be fictional. Whatever the origins of the term, it was soon replaced with the more pragmatic SONAR (SOund NAvigation and Ranging). SONAR can be used in 'active' or 'passive' mode.

Passive SONAR systems and hydrophones can be used to listen for sounds around the boat and to build up a picture of what is going on outside. Passive SONAR does not, by definition, have emissions that can be picked up by another vessel. This makes it a useful way to search for hostile craft while (hopefully) remaining undetected. All vessels make at least some noise that can be detected by a sensitive-enough passive SONAR unit.

Reducing noise is an important part of submarine design as it both reduces the chances of being detected and increases the effectiveness of on-board SONAR units. Under normal conditions a submarine will make a certain amount of noise, but this can be reduced by shutting down non-essential systems, moving slowly and avoiding accidental

RIGHT: The periscope allows a submarine to observe above the surface without exposing itself.

noise. The latter can be caused by crew activity ranging from talking, to metal tools striking against the submarine's components. The term 'silent running' refers to the strenuous attempts made by early submariners to eliminate noise during combat conditions.

Active SONAR emits sound pulses (the distinctive 'pings' forever associated with submarines) and detects their return. Sound propagates well through water and is reflected by objects. Active SONAR can be used for navigation, seabed mapping and fish-finding as well as searching for a target to attack. It does, however, announce the presence of the emitting vessel to any hostiles in the area.

Using SONAR is anything but simple. Temperature variations and changes in pressure and salinity in the water cause

sound waves to distort and sometimes even reflect them. One of the most important underwater features to a SONAR operator is the Thermocline, or 'the layer'. This is an inversion layer where water at different temperatures meets. The sudden change in water density is small but can be enough to bounce sound waves off, rather than allow them to continue in a straight line.

The Thermocline can hide a vessel by bouncing SONAR pulses emitted on the other side of the layer, or it can allow a target to be detected at great distances due to what is known as a Convergence Zone, again caused by reflection of sound

BELOW: A crewman operates SONAR aboard the *Ohio* class guided missile submarine USS *Florida* in May 2006.

waves. Thus interpretation of SONAR data is a complex business. Drawing the right conclusions can be a matter of life and death to naval submariners (see pp70–71 for more on SONAR).

Submarine Weapons

Although the ability to travel underwater allowed submarines to approach other vessels undetected for an attack, the question of how to make that attack was a tricky one. Early submarines could not mount cannon on deck, so some other means had to be found.

One option was to use the submarine to sneak close to an enemy vessel and attach an explosive charge with a timed detonator. This was risky, but offered an inferior navy the chance to strike at a more powerful force.

Once guns were invented that fired an all-in-one shell and were not so prone to wetness, submarines became capable of mounting a useful gun armament. Up until the end of World War II, submarines often engaged their targets on the surface with deck guns. However, this practice was never very efficient and modern submarines use underwater weapons only. Some can lay mines, but the usual weapon is the torpedo. The term 'torpedo' was originally applied to the weapon that we now call a mine, but with the invention of the 'automotive torpedo', the term was hijacked to refer to the self-propelled weapon we know today.

Torpedoes deliver an explosive charge at a distance. Depending on the type, they may attempt a contact explosion or detonate under the target vessel. Originally torpedoes were unguided and not very reliable, but gradually a range of homing and guided torpedoes were developed that allowed an attack to be made with precision, from very far off. Torpedoes are not much faster than most surface vessels, so an attack with unguided torpedoes is a tricky business. It is necessary to calculate where the

target will be when the torpedoes arrive and aim for that point. This is termed a 'firing solution'. The solution can be ruined if the target ship changes course, resulting in a miss. Modern torpedoes either home in on the target, or else can be guided by signals fed down a fibre-optic cable from the launching vessel.

Some submarines can launch missiles, either from their torpedo tubes or from compartments in the hull. The weapons themselves range from short-range, anti-

ABOVE: A Trident submarine-launched missile. The chief advantage of a submarine-mounted nuclear arsenal is that launch platforms are very difficult to locate.

ship missiles through to cruise missiles for land attack and intercontinental ballistic missiles. There are also anti-aircraft missile systems available for submarines, allowing an anti-submarine helicopter to be attacked if this is a better option than trying to sneak away (see pp68–69 for more on weapons).

RIGHT: The MK37 torpedo (top) and the Stingray torpedo. The Stingray has a unique guidance system and a high single-shot kill probability.

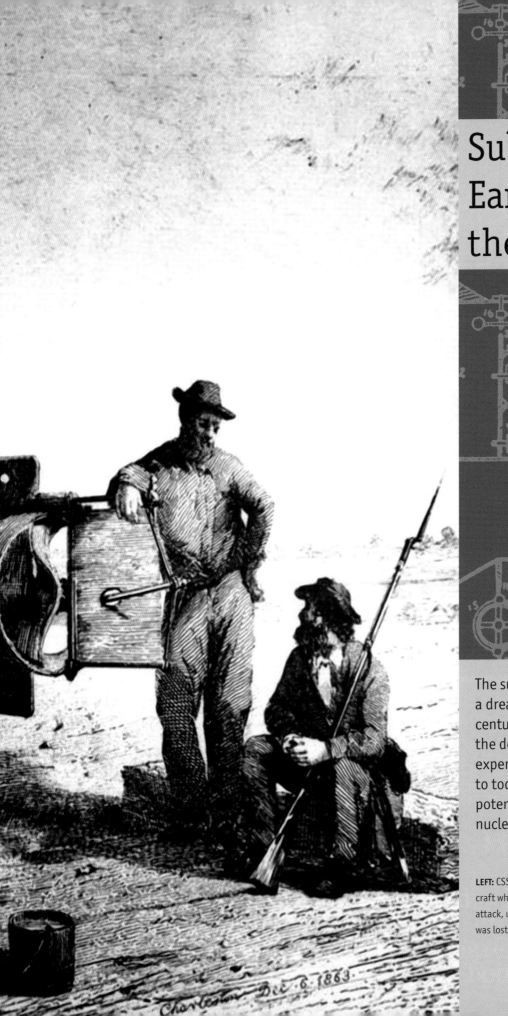

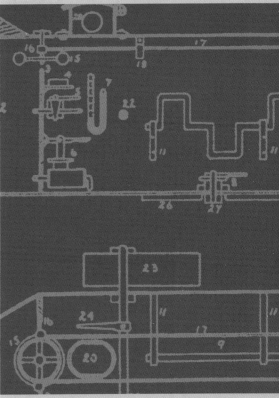

Submarines from Early Times to the Present Day

The submarine had been a dream of inventors for centuries. This book follows the development of the first experimental submarines, to today's modern and potentially devastating nuclear submarines.

LEFT: CSS *Hunley* was a manually-propelled craft which made the world's first successful attack, using a spar torpedo. *Hunley* herself was lost in the attempt.

Early Experiments

First Attempts

In 1580, William Bourne wrote a scientific account of how a boat floated. Based on this thesis he also presented a theory of how a craft might be made to submerge and rise again under control.

Less than 50 years later, in 1623, a submersible boat was built and demonstrated by Cornelius Drebbel. Apparently Drebbel took a boat suitable to carry a crew of twelve men and enclosed it to create a watertight craft. It is not known how Drebbel dealt with the problem of buoyancy. The most likely theory is that the boat had slightly positive buoyancy and was driven down by hydroplanes of a sort while in motion. Drebbel was able to demonstrate his boat on the River Thames at a depth of about 5m (16ft).

The Rotterdam Boat

Other experiments included the 1653 Rotterdam Boat, which was an attempt to build the world's first military submersible. It was a roughly cylindrical vessel with tapered ends, making it reasonably well streamlined for underwater movement. The Rotterdam Boat did not carry any weapons but was designed to attack an enemy vessel by ramming it just below the waterline. The boat had a clever and innovative clockwork propulsion system but this was not powerful enough to move the vessel, let alone generate enough momentum for a ramming attack.

LEFT: Cornelius Drebbel built three manually-powered submarines which he successfully demonstrated on the Thames.

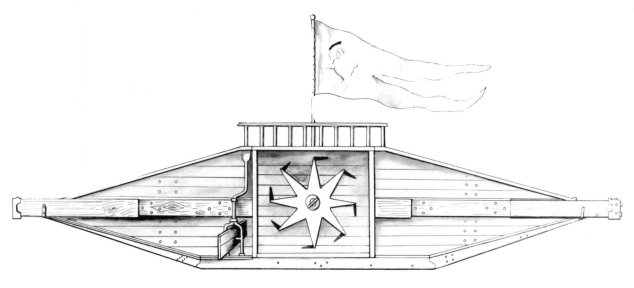

BOTTOM: The Rotterdam Boat was intended to sink enemy vessels by ramming them, but its powerplant could not generate enough power.

A Bold Concept

The less dramatic but more practical *Turtle*, invented by David Bushnell, was in many ways the typical expedient of a weak naval power facing a much stronger one. It was a bold, unconventional concept that would not have even been considered by a major naval power. *Turtle* relied on stealth and surprise to make its attack, which was to be carried out by getting underneath an anchored warship and attaching a timed charge contained in a watertight barrel towed by the craft.

Turtle was a barrel-shaped vessel propelled by two hand-cranked screws. It was designed to remain submerged a little below the surface and controlled its depth with a vertical screw. Horizontal movement was provided by the second screw, with guidance from the craft's small rudder. In 1776, *Turtle* attacked a British warship in New York harbour but was unable to attach the charge. However, the craft and its intrepid operator, Sergeant Ezra Lee, did make their escape.

Basic Principles

The early inventors understood the basic principles of the naval submarine, even if the technology to build an effective one did not at the time exist. Their boats solved the problems of buoyancy control in two ways: controllable ballast and the use of hydroplanes as a sort of rudder for vertical direction. Both of these methods are still in use today, albeit in an immensely refined form.

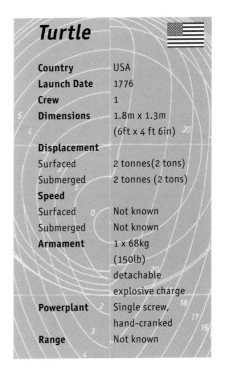

Turtle 🇺🇸	
Country	USA
Launch Date	1776
Crew	1
Dimensions	1.8m x 1.3m
	(6ft x 4 ft 6in)
Displacement	
Surfaced	2 tonnes(2 tons)
Submerged	2 tonnes (2 tons)
Speed	
Surfaced	Not known
Submerged	Not known
Armament	1 x 68kg
	(150lb)
	detachable
	explosive charge
Powerplant	Single screw,
	hand-cranked
Range	Not known

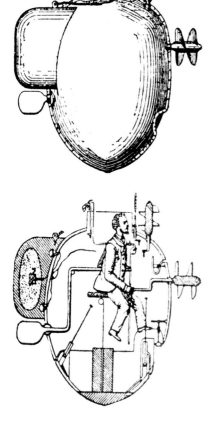

BELOW: The *Turtle*, although primitive in the extreme, was the world's first workable combat submarine.

The hull was ballasted to have neutral buoyancy, floating just below the surface.

Small portholes provided the operator with a very limited view of his surroundings, making moving difficult.

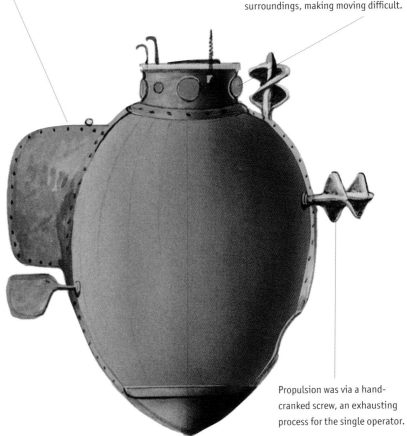

Propulsion was via a hand-cranked screw, an exhausting process for the single operator.

Nineteenth-century Developments

The name *Nautilus* is popularly associated with submarines thanks to the fiction of Jules Verne, but the first *Nautilus* was built by Robert Fulton for the French navy. He offered to operate *Nautilus* as a privateer in return for a bounty paid per enemy vessel sunk.

Nautilus was capable of about 4 knots and operated at a depth of up to 6m (19ft). It could remain submerged for up to six hours, obtaining air by means of hoses attached to a floating buoy on the surface. *Nautilus* had a sail for use on the surface and was intended to attack by attaching an explosive charge. *Nautilus* seemed promising in trials and had some interesting features, including the ability to trim the boat by pumping air into water-filled ballast tanks. However, during several attempted attacks on British vessels, the craft was easily evaded and the French navy lost interest. Fulton offered *Nautilus* to the British instead, who were equally unimpressed.

Brandtaucher

The submarine *Brandtaucher* was created to attack the Danish fleet, then blockading Kiel. It was built of iron and propelled by men walking in treadmills. On its first outing *Brandtaucher* was marginally successful – Danish warships retreated when it appeared – but on its second voyage the boat went out of control and became stuck in mud on the bottom. *Brandtaucher*'s crew escaped by waiting for pressure to equalise inside the vessel so that the hatch

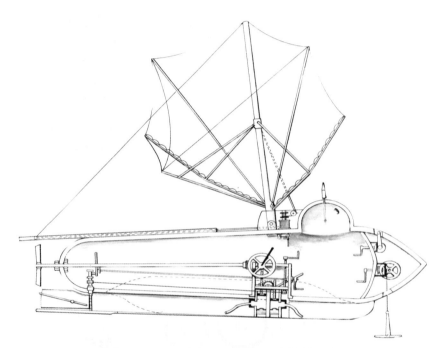

ABOVE: *Nautilus* was a step in the right direction, and demonstrated several important concepts such as water-filled ballast tanks.

BELOW: The *Intelligent Whale* demonstrated the ability to convey a diver close to the target, which was then attacked with a demolition charge.

could be forced open, and swam to the surface some 10m (30ft) above.

Somewhat more successful was *Diable Marin*, which was demonstrated on over 100 occasions. It could accommodate 16 people and once carried a small brass band, which played the Russian national anthem in honour of the Tzar's birthday. Other experiments did not go so well. In 1863, the French boat *Le Plongeur*, powered by compressed air, was tested but turned out to be uncontrollable. The US equivalent, named *Intelligent Whale*, foundered on the rocks of legality. No-one in the USA was prepared to authorize the project for many years and its inventor was murdered before trials were completed.

ABOVE: Fulton designed a second *Nautilus*, essentially a small conventional vessel which could submerge.

Propulsion was by a single screw, enabling an underwater top speed of 3 knots.

A conning tower-like structure at the fore end of *Brandtaucher* contained the entry hatch.

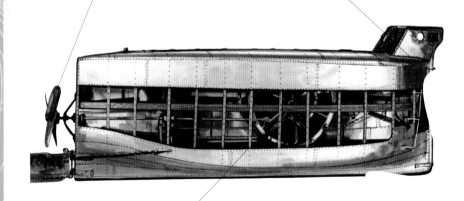

Manually-powered treadmills for propulsion required a large, high boat to accommodate them.

Nautilus

Country	USA
Launch Date	1800
Crew	3
Dimensions	6.4m x 1.2m (21ft x 3ft 7in)
Displacement	19 tonnes (18.7 tons)
Speed	Not known
Armament	Single detachable explosive charge
Powerplant	Single screw, hand-cranked
Range	Not known

Submarines of the American Civil War

The American Civil War was the first conflict in which submarines played a serious part. They were very much weapons of desperation and were thus used by the Confederacy. The Union had little interest in such novelties.

The Union continued with the policy of the US Navy, which had rejected a prototype submarine in 1852. Its caustic assertion was that the navy used boats that floated on water, rather than sinking under it. The Confederacy could not afford such sentiments. It was under blockade by a greatly superior naval force and needed to even the odds somehow. If submarines were useful in breaking the blockade then they would be employed. The Confederacy thus issued permission for submarines to be operated as privateers by anyone who could build one. A bounty would be paid for any Union vessel sunk.

Hand-propelled

The first attempt was *Pioneer*, developed by Horace Hunley. A three-man, hand-propelled submarine, *Pioneer* was successfully demonstrated, managing to sink a target barge by towing a floating charge into proximity. However, *Pioneer* was scuttled when New Orleans fell to the Union. A slightly different approach created the *David*, a small vessel designed to sink the 'Goliath' of a major warship. The *David* was not a submarine but attacked awash, hoping to avoid detection by being very low in the water. The usual weapon was a spar torpedo – a charge on the end of a long pole, which was rammed against the side of an enemy vessel. The *David* made several attacks but achieved little success.

CSS *Hunley*

Hunley tried again with a larger boat, which was created out of an iron boiler. Propelled by eight men cranking a hand-powered propeller and a ninth man steering, this boat had only one means of entry or egress, a small hatch on the

topside. The boat sank several times, killing Hunley himself. With remarkable persistence, the survivors kept experimenting with the boat every time it was raised, eventually renaming it CSS *Hunley*. Despite being informed that their contraption was far too hazardous for any enterprise, the crew demanded permission to try again. This time, CSS *Hunley* attacked just awash rather than submerged, using a spar torpedo. As *Hunley* approached her target, USS *Housatonic*, she was spotted by a US naval ensign who gained the dubious distinction of being the first man killed by enemy action from a submarine. He was shot with a shotgun from *Hunley*'s open hatch. The attack was then made and *Housatonic* was sunk, but *Hunley* herself also foundered.

MAIN IMAGE: *Davids* were not true submarines as they attacked awash rather than underwater.

BELOW: A depiction of the attack by CSS *Hunley* against USS *Housatonic*.

CSS *David*

Country	CSA
Launch Date	1863
Crew	5
Dimensions	15.2m x 1.8m x 1.5m (50ft x 6ft x 5ft)
Displacement	Not known
Speed	Not known
Armament	1 spar torpedo
Powerplant	Steam engine
Range	Not known

Towards the Modern Submarine

In 1869, the United States Navy obtained a licence to build the Whitehead Automotive Torpedo, which finally gave submarines a credible attack capability. At much the same time, the idea of powering a submarine using the internal combustion engine began to catch on.

It was still some time before a workable design for the internal combustion engine emerged. In the meantime, publication of Jules Verne's *20,000 Leagues Under The Sea* began to popularize the submarine as a vessel of war. Experimentation with powered submarines gathered pace in the late nineteenth century. Claude Goubert tried to build an electric boat, while Josiah Tuck built a steam boat powered by chemicals rather that a furnace. This vessel, named *Resurgam*, stored steam under pressure to power its underwater movement. A promising design, *Resurgam* sank while being towed on the surface.

Steam-powered

A slightly more successful steam-powered boat, armed with a single torpedo, was built by Nordenfeldt. It was developed from the *Resurgam* design. Nordenfeldt's boat was bought by the Greek navy but proved extremely difficult to control. When the improved prototype *Nordenfeldt II* sank on trials and *Nordenfeldt III* ran aground en route to delivery, the concept quietly faded from the scene. Meanwhile, Gustave Zede's boat *Gymnote* demonstrated that electric power was workable. However, *Gymnote* could not recharge its batteries, so it remained a technology demonstrator only. Nevertheless, Zede earned himself a place in the annals of submarine design and later boats were named in his honour. One solution to the battery-

Gustave Zede

Country	France
Launch Date	June 1893
Crew	19
Dimensions	48.5m x 3.2m x 3.2m (159ft x 10ft 6in x 10ft 6in)
Displacement	
Surfaced	265 tonnes (261 tons)
Submerged	274 tonnes (270 tons)
Speed	
Surfaced	20 knots
Submerged	28 knots
Armament	1 x 450mm (17.7in) torpedo tube
Powerplant	Single screw, electric motor
Range	Not known

RIGHT: Named after her inventor, *Gustave Zede* was probably the first submarine to mount an effective periscope.

charging problem was demonstrated by George Baker's experimental vessel, which used a steam engine to drive a dynamo and thus keep the batteries topped up. Other novel designs included *Argonaut*, which had wheels to allow it to drive on the bottom when necessary.

Modern Boats

At the very end of the century, modern boats began to emerge. The French boat *Gustave Zede* was able to conduct a successful torpedo attack on exercise, which prompted interest in a true military submarine. It also managed over 2500 dives without meeting with disaster. *Gustave Zede* was important in other ways too – she had a conning tower atop where lookouts could stand when she surfaced, and a central control room just beneath it. *Gustave Zede* was followed by *Narval*, which used a diesel engine.

ABOVE: *Argonaut* survived in the open sea in a storm that sank many other vessels. The designer was congratulated in a letter from Jules Verne.

ABOVE RIGHT: *Gymnote* made over 2000 dives under electric power, proving the concept for later, more developed vessels. She eventually sank at Toulon in 1907.

Holland's Boats

The name of John Holland is prominently associated with submarines. Holland started out with a proposal to the US Navy for a boat, which was rejected. His ideas were taken up by the Fenians – Irish rebels who were willing to support Holland's experiments.

Holland 1

The first Holland boat was named *Holland 1* and worked well enough that a larger vessel was constructed for combat purposes. This was *Fenian Ram* and seemed promising. However, the project collapsed in internal bickering. Undeterred, Holland formed his own company and built a submarine named the *Zalinski Boat*. It was damaged at launch and the project collapsed along with the company. Next, Holland entered a US navy design competition and won it, only to have the project derailed twice by political decisions. Finally, he obtained funding to build *Plunger*, a torpedo-armed boat that the Navy insisted must be steam-powered. This made the boat too hot for the crew. Holland had argued strenuously against steam power but was overruled by naval officers who had no experience with submarines and – according to Holland – lacked the slightest understanding of how to build one.

Plunger was followed by the gasoline-engined *Holland VI*, which mounted a compressed-air-powered dynamite gun as well as a single torpedo. The *Holland VI* design was bought by the US Navy, and other navies began placing orders for small numbers. Among those impressed by the boats' performance was Admiral Sir John 'Jacky' Fisher, who for a time advocated a navy made up entirely of submarines and torpedo boats. However, the US Navy remained dubious. Some officers saw the boats as mere novelties while others speculated that had the enemy possessed submarines in the recent US-Spanish war, they might have prevented the capture of Manila.

Legal Challenges

Holland had formed several companies to build submarines, but just as he finally achieved success with the Electric Boat Company, he was edged out by internal politics. Holland made one final attempt and sold some improved designs but was put out of business by legal challenges from Electric Boat.

RIGHT: John Philip Holland spent most of his working life developing submarines. Much of his research was funded by the Fenian Brotherhood, who hoped to create a weapon to be used against Britain.

Holland VI	🇺🇸
Country	USA
Launch Date	May 1897
Crew	7
Dimensions	16.3m x 3.1m x 3.5m (53ft 3in x 10ft 3in x 11ft 6in)
Displacement	
Surfaced	64 tonnes (63 tons)
Submerged	76 tonnes (75 tons)
Speed	
Surfaced	8 knots
Submerged	5 knots
Armament	1 x 457mm (18in) torpedo tube; 1 x pneumatic gun
Powerplant	Single screw, petrol engine/electric motor
Range	Submerged: 74km (40nm) at 3 knots

The *Holland VI* had a streamlined hull form that allowed a top speed of 5 knots underwater, or 8 knots on the surface.

Armament included one 457mm (18in) torpedo tube and a pneumatic gun.

Operating the boat and its weapons required a crew of seven.

RIGHT: *Holland 1* was the first submarine commissioned by the Royal Navy; she was the first of six boats in the *Holland* class.

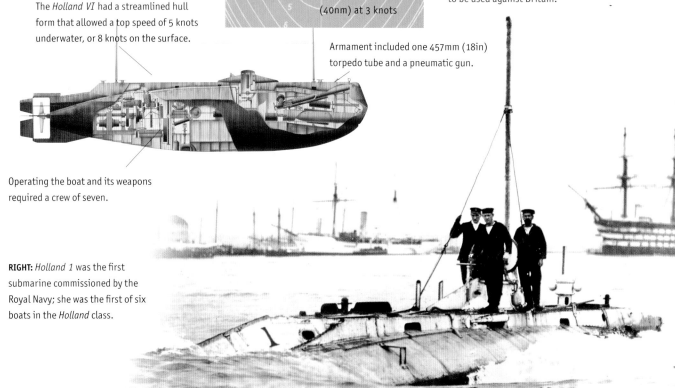

World War I Era

First Attempts

Although the submarine was a technology in its infancy at the dawn of the twentieth century, it was sufficiently promising that the British and French navies were already fielding them in numbers; albeit with some reservations about how they might be used.

Early boats such as the British 'A' class, which were slightly improved *Holland VI*s, possessed very limited capabilities. The 'A' class which were launched between 1902 and 1905, mounted only a single torpedo (with no reload capability) and had a short operational range. However, experience was gained with these boats and the 'B' class which followed, benefited from better shape, improved handling and a doubled armament. Operational range was five times as great.

Attack in Home Waters

There were those who thought that submarines were useful only for coastal

RIGHT: USS *Seal* was constructed to meet a set of requirements which were far in excess of what seemed possible, yet met or exceeded them all. In 1914 she set a depth record at 256ft (78m).

USS *Seal*

Country	USA
Launch Date	1911
Crew	24
Dimensions	49m x 4m x 3.7m (161 x 13ft.1in x 12ft 2in)
Displacement	
Surfaced	406 tonnes (400 tons)
Submerged	524 tonnes (516 tons)
Speed	
Surfaced	14 knots
Submerged	10 knots
Armament	Four 18-inch bow torpedo tubes in a trainable deck mount, two bow tubes
Powerplant	Unknown
Range	Unknown

defence, while others believed that they might be able to make a stealthy attack on an enemy even in his home waters. This concept was demonstrated in a 1910 exercise, when a British 'D' class submarine successfully attacked two cruisers as they left port. One idea for using submarines was to try to draw the enemy into a pursuit, which would lead him into a submarine ambush. This tactic was attempted in both World Wars, and the fear that submarines might be lurking ahead caused some commanders to be unduly cautious.

The general idea prevailing at the time was that the submarine was a warship like any other, and would be used in fleet operations or for attacks on enemy naval assets. The concept of using submarines as commerce raiders was questionable, to say the least. International law required that fair warning be given before a merchant ship was attacked, which meant that the submarine had to surface. This robbed it of its main advantage – stealth – and rendered it extremely vulnerable to enemy action.

ABOVE: The 'D' class boats were Britain's first true ocean-going submarines rather than short-range harbour-protection vessels.

Despite this lack of a clear mission, submarine development continued. In 1914, USS *Seal* set a depth record of 256 feet (78m), but the biggest step forward was the adoption of a diesel system to replace the usual petrol engine. This removed the danger of explosion posed by sparks from electrical equipment in an atmosphere laden with petrol vapour. The first US diesel sub was assigned to Lieutenant (who later became Admiral) Chester Nimitz.

German Submarines of Early World War I

It was not until 1906 that

Germany obtained its first Unterzeeboot, or U-Boat. *U-1* was a credible weapon of war, capable of 8.7 knots underwater and 10.8 knots on the surface using kerosene engines. Armament was modest; a single torpedo tube, but *U-1* could cruise about 2845km (1536nm) on the surface. Germany started late with submarines but benefited from the experience of others. From the first, all German boats had twin screws powered by kerosene engines rather than the more dangerous petrol systems favoured elsewhere. Double hulls – an inner pressure hull and an outer hull carrying components that did not need to be protected from pressure – were used on all vessels.

By the outbreak of World War I, U-boats were an effective weapon. Typical armament included four 508mm (20in) torpedo tubes and an 86mm (3.4in) deck gun. Development continued at a steady pace. *U-21*, built in 1913, was about two and a half times the size of *U-1* and had a cruising range of 10,186km (5500nm). In 1915, *UB-14* scored a notable first – the sinking of another submarine. This was the British *E20*, which was ambushed in the Sea of Marmara. *E20* was on the surface at the time she was attacked. Documents captured aboard a French submarine indicated the rendezvous area used by British and French boats, allowing an attack to be set up.

Rules of Engagement

U-boats sank a number of major naval vessels, including the destruction of an entire cruiser squadron in the North Sea by *U-9*. The fear of submarine attack heavily influenced British naval thinking at sea and even prompted the fleet to move from Scapa Flow to safer bases on the west side of Scotland.

ABOVE: The *U-35* was the most successful submarine of World War I. She sank over 200 Allied ships from 1915–1918.

Deutschland	
Country	Germany
Launch Date	1916
Crew	56
Dimensions	65m x 8.9m x 5.3m (213ft 3in x 29ft 2in x 17ft 5in)
Displacement	
Surfaced	1536 tonnes (1512 tons)
Submerged	1905 tonnes (1875 tons)
Speed	
Surfaced	12.4 knots
Submerged	5.2 knots
Armament	None
Powerplant	Twin screw diesel engines, electric motors
Range	20,909km (11,280nm)

Deutschland could make 12.4 knots on the surface, comparable with many conventional merchant vessels.

As a warship, *U-155* carried 18 torpedoes launched from two bow tubes. She was not armed whilst serving as a merchant vessel.

Deutschland was essentially a blockade runner which could submerge to sneak past patrols.

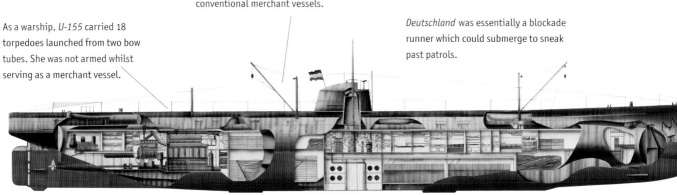

U-boats also carried out commerce raiding against merchant traffic. At first, efforts were made to comply with international law, but excessive U-boat losses prompted a number of changes in the rules of engagement (and some guidance to U-boat skippers on creative log entries) to allow boats to operate at reduced risk by using surprise attacks. It became apparent that the only viable strategy was to use unrestricted submarine warfare, sinking merchant ships without warning. By this time the Allied blockade of Germany was causing severe shortages, and it was felt to be morally acceptable to do the same to Britain by any means necessary.

Submarine Innovations

At the beginning of the war, no means existed to track or attack a submerged submarine, but necessity forced the rapid development of technology. Surface ships were outfitted with depth charges and forward-firing mortars launching contact-fused projectiles. Attacks were guided by ASDIC – the rather primitive forerunner of today's SONAR system. Although these innovations gave the anti-submarine forces the ability to strike back, German submarines continued to take a toll of merchant traffic.

RIGHT: Since few torpedoes could be carried, most submarine attacks were made on the surface using deck guns.

Allied Submarines of Early World War I

Some Allied nations entered the war with large submarine fleets. Most vessels were very basic, such as the British 'A' and 'B' classes, and were of limited effectiveness. The 'D' class was the first British submarine intended for more than local coastal operations, and the 'E' class had an operational range of 6628km (3579nm).

'D' class boats helped protect troop convoys to the Continent and made offensive patrols into the Heligoland Bight. These boats were easier to operate and less prone to problems than their predecessors. Equally importantly, they could send wireless transmissions. This made them useful reconnaissance assets and permitted cooperation with surface vessels.

As the war went on, armament gradually increased with boats gaining more torpedo tubes. It became standard practice to mount rearward-facing torpedo tubes, giving the commander extra options. Underwater reloading of torpedo tubes was a relatively new technique and took considerable time, so most boats could only launch as many torpedoes as they had tubes in any one attack. Despite earlier commanders labelling the submarine as 'unfair' and 'un-English', British boats were aggressively handled and enjoyed considerable success against enemy shipping, including capital vessels such as the Turkish battleship *Hairredin Barbarossa*.

European Efforts

France started the war with 62 submarines, many of which were active in the Mediterranean and the Adriatic. In April 1916, a *Frimaire* class boat sneaked into an Austrian harbour to torpedo a destroyer. Italian boats also took on the Austro-Hungarian navy in the Adriatic. They were small and had a short range and tended to operate on the defensive as a result.

Russian Submarines

Russia started the war with nearly 50 boats. Many were of very early designs, such as Holland and Lake class boats with minimal armament. Russian submarines were active in the Baltic Sea before the Russian Revolution took the country out of the war. Italy's submarine force was mainly confined to Adriatic operations, attempting to keep the Austro-Hungarian fleet bottled up. The shallow waters of the Adriatic were difficult territory for submarines, and it was soon discovered that a sub could be spotted from the air. However, at the time there was no air-dropped weapon to attack a submerged boat.

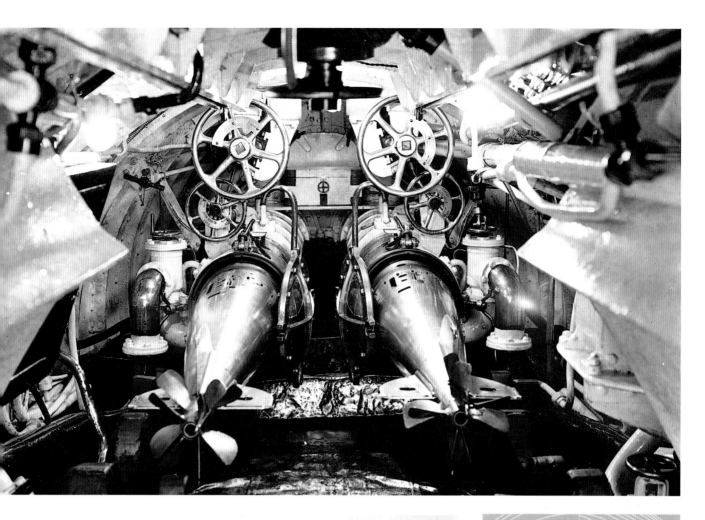

TOP LEFT: Britain's larger 'D' and 'E' class vessels were aggressively handled and achieved notable successes during the war.

ABOVE: *Ventose*, a boat of the French *Pluviose* class. These vessels were steam-powered.

TOP: Torpedoes aboard a British 'E' class boat. Some 55 'E' class boats were constructed, of which six could carry mines instead of part of their torpedo armament.

'E' Class

Country	United Kingdom
Launch Date	1913
Crew	30
Dimensions	55.17m x 6.91m x 3.81m (181ft, 22ft 8in x 12ft 6in)
Displacement	
Surfaced	677 tonnes (666 tons)
Submerged	820 tonnes (807 tons)
Speed	
Surfaced	14 knots
Submerged	9 knots
Armament	5 x 457mm (18in) torpedo tubes; 1 x 12-pounder gun
Powerplant	Two twin-shaft diesel engines, two electric motors
Range	6628km (3579nm)

German Submarines of Late World War I

Germany was under blockade, more or less, from the beginning of the war, and attempted to use its submarine fleet to impose a similar position on Britain. Surface attacks made with due warning resulted in unacceptable casualties at the hands of surface warships rushing to aid the merchant, or the guns of Q-ships.

Q-ships were merchantmen armed with concealed guns, and they succeeded in attacking a number of U-boats by surprise during the war. An attempt was made to create a compromise between the letter of international law and the practicalities of submarine warfare. Zones were declared in which any ship was subject to attack without any further warning. However, this was not enough – the only viable strategy was to attack without regard to conventions or laws that had been drawn up with surface vessels in mind.

Unrestricted Warfare

Once the policy of unrestricted submarine warfare was in place, the U-boats were much more effective, coming close to starving Britain into submission. However, the policy also helped bring America into the war and sealed the fate of the Central Powers. In many ways the imposition of all-out submarine warfare was the turning point of the war. There was a real chance that it might bring victory, but the risks were considerable. The boats making these attacks were a mix of upgraded early-war designs, some mounting guns of up to 127mm (5in) calibre, and newly built vessels. These included long-range submarine cruisers, able to make 15 knots on the surface to get into position for an attack and carrying enough torpedoes for an extended war patrol.

New Weapons

At first, a submarine that could dive in time was safe from retaliation, but gradually new weapons emerged including depth charges and contact-detonated weapons that were dropped

U-139

Country	Germany
Launch Date	1917
Crew	62
Dimensions	94.8m x 9m x 5.2m (311ft x 29ft 9in x 17ft 3in)
Displacement	
Surfaced	1961 tonnes (1930 tons)
Submerged	2523 tonnes (2483 tons)
Speed	
Surfaced	15.8 knots
Submerged	7.6 knots
Armament	6 x 508mm (20in) torpedo tubes; 2 x 150mm (5.9in) guns
Powerplant	Twin shafts, diesel/ electric motors
Range	23,391km (12,630nm)

in a pattern over the boat's suspected position. These were assisted by underwater detection systems such as ASDIC (now known as SONAR) and radio direction-finding techniques to located subs by their transmissions to base.

Improved Tactics

In addition to their weapons the Allies also improved their tactics. Convoy escorts tried to sink any U-boats they sighted, but the key to victory lay in getting supplies across the Atlantic rather than inflicting losses on the enemy fleet. A U-boat that was forced down while the convoy passed would not usually be able to catch up. This was a victory for the escorts, albeit a less than glamorous one.

BELOW: *U-139*, a large 'submarine cruiser'. These boats were intended to act mainly as submersible surface combatants but arrived too late to have any impact on the course of the war.

Great War Experiments

Although submarines were fighting World War I as best they could, nobody really knew what they were capable of. Experimentation went on in several nations, often without success. The German Navy experimented with seaplane-carrying submarines, and others followed suit. The basic idea was sound – the sub would get the aircraft safely to its patrol area and provide what was effectively an air base in the middle of the sea. At this point the aircraft could be used for reconnaissance to find targets for the submarine, or for a surface fleet.

RIGHT: The crew of *Deutschland*. Submarines were used to carry supplies and high-value raw materials during both World Wars, but have never entered widespread commercial use.

BELOW: British submarine *M2* was converted from a big-gun vessel to a submarine aircraft carrier.

However, there were some serious practical problems.

Vulnerable Aircraft

Aircraft had to be carried dismantled and assembled before flight, which left the submarine vulnerable during that period. Getting the aircraft back in the hangar after its mission was also a lengthy process. If hostile surface units appeared on the scene and the boat had to dive, the aircraft would be stranded far from home. Germany also built the world's first cargo-carrying submarines, *Deutschland* and *Oldenburg*, which made voyages to New York before being converted to a combat role. Although the cargo subs could not carry much, they were able to slip past the Allied

blockade of the German coast and bring in much-needed supplies. *Deutschland* made two runs to New York before America entered the war, at which point she was converted to a fighting U-boat.

'K' class

The British wanted a very fast submarine that could operate with battlecruisers,

'K' Class	
Country	United Kingdom
Launch Date	1916
Crew	50–60
Dimensions	100.6m x 8.1m x 5.2m (330ft x 26ft 7in x 17ft)
Displacement	
Surfaced	2174 tonnes (2140 tons)
Submerged	2814 tonnes (2770 tons)
Speed	
Surfaced	23 knots
Submerged	9 knots
Armament	10 x 533mm (21in) torpedo tubes; 3 x 102mm (4in) guns
Powerplant	Twin screws, steam turbines/electric motors
Range	5556km (3000nm)

and so in 1913 an outline design was prepared for the 'K' class. K-boats were steam-powered in order to maintain the very high surface speeds necessary, and this resulted in a large boat that gave up much of its tonnage to engines. The K-boats were very difficult to control; so much so that five were lost to accidents, most notably in the notorious 'Battle of May Island'. This chaotic incident took place entirely without an enemy presence – a hurried course change to avoid a collision resulted in the uncontrollable boats ramming one another. Early models

were also prone to violently pitching down when diving; it was possible for the bows to pass crush depth with the stern out of the water. Later, some of the K-boats were converted to carry huge 305mm (12in) guns as the 'M' class. These vessels were to bombard coastal targets or attack enemy shipping with gunfire.

ABOVE: HMS *M-1*, an experimental big-gun submarine. Originally intended for coastal bombardment.

The steam-powered 'K' class were notoriously hard to control. The class was used as the basis for the experimental 'M' class.

The funnels folded flat when diving, contributing to a lamentable dive time.

The curious flared bow was added in an effort to control downward pitching.

Allied Submarines of Late World War I

Allied submarines also improved during the course of the war, becoming faster and more capable. The British 'J' class was designed as a counter to fast German subs, and could make 17 knots on the surface.

The 'J' class had six torpedo tubes and a 75mm (2.95in) gun. Few were built, but their capabilities were demonstrated when *J1* torpedoed two German battleships. In addition to surface vessel kills, British submarines sank 17 German boats, and achieved the distinction of making the first sub-on-sub kill while both vessels were submerged. This required inventing a technique for calculating a three-dimensional torpedo-firing solution in the middle of combat.

Hunter-killers

A specialist sub-hunting submarine was developed. This was the 'R' class. Small and fast, equipped with specialist sensors and armed only with torpedoes, these craft were not available early enough to make a difference, but they showed the way for the future. They can be considered the first 'Hunter-Killer' submarines.

US Designs

The USA entered World War I with 30 submarines in service. By the end of the war there were 120. US boats did not contribute greatly to the war effort, though the submarine service gained considerable experience that proved useful in World War II. Some of the US designs were fairly poor. Most still used petrol engines which were a constant explosion hazard. Others were either obsolete by the time they entered service, like USS *Seal*, or difficult to operate. The latter included a number of boats designed by the Italian Laurenti, which also posed problems for the builders. Conversely, some US designs were both innovative and useful. Among them was the 'L' class, which had a retractable deck gun. This reduced underwater drag and permitted a slightly higher submerged speed than otherwise. The same class demonstrated the need for US boats to be able to dive faster – the 'L' class took nearly two and a half minutes to submerge. US designers had not greatly worried about diving speed up to this point. The theory was that the masts of a warship could be seen far enough away to allow a leisurely dive. The advent of aircraft, coupled with operational experience under wartime conditions, changed this view and subsequent classes paid more attention to diving speed.

RIGHT: Sailors drill with the 12-pounder gun aboard a British 'E' class boat.

BELOW: *L-10*, a late-war British boat, sank a German destroyer in October 1918 but was then sunk by other surface vessels.

ABOVE: Two 'R' class and one 'H' class boats. The 'R' class was the world's first 'Hunter-Killer' submarine, designed to locate and sink U-boats.

USS *L-10*

Country	USA
Launch Date	March 1916
Crew	28 officers and men
Dimensions	51.03m x 5.31m x 4.14m (167ft 5in x 17ft 5in x 13ft 7in)
Displacement	
Surfaced	457 tonnes (450 tons)
Submerged	557tonnes (548 tons)
Speed	
Surfaced	14 knots
Submerged	10.5 knots
Armament	1 x 76mm (3in) gun; 4 x 457mm (18in) torpedo tubes
Powerplant	Twin screws, diesel/ electric motors
Range	8334km (4500nm)

World War II Era

First Attempts

By the end of World War I, the submarine had proved itself as a credible weapon system, and its role was now properly understood. Gunfire was to be used against minor targets or to finish off a crippled vessel, but it was as a delivery system for the torpedo that the submarine excelled. Torpedo attacks could be made on the surface or from underwater. One anti-convoy technique was to get inside the convoy at night and attack on the surface. The submarine's low profile made it very hard to spot and often the escorts would go haring off into the darkness searching for an external threat, while the sub made use of its surfaced speed to remain with the convoy and set up another attack. Experiments were carried out with other weapon systems. Mine-laying submarines had proven workable in World War I and some designs carried mines in addition to their other armament. Mines could be carried outside the pressure hull and deployed stealthily, ideally in a harbour mouth or similar choke point.

French Design

Other experiments were not so successful. Among them was *Surcouf*, a French submarine armed with twin 203mm (8in) guns in a large turret on the front of the conning tower. The British had flirted with big-gun submarines in the form of the 'M' class, finding them unworkable, but the French design was more promising. *Surcouf* could engage very rapidly after surfacing and might have made an effective raider. However, she was lost in collision with a freighter and never saw action.

BELOW: The US *M-1* was an experimental vessel, testing concepts such as a double hull and new electric batteries. She was the forerunner of World War II submarines.

USS *M-1*

Country	USA
Launch Date	1915
Crew	28
Dimensions	58.75m x 4.49m
	(192ft 9in x 14ft 9in)
Displacement	
Surfaced	480 tonnes (472 tons)
Submerged	665 tonnes (654 tons)
Speed	
Surfaced	14 knots
Submerged	10.5 knots
Armament	4 x 457mm (18in)
	torpedo tubes; 8 x
	torpedoes; 1 x 76mm
	(3in) deck gun
Powerplant	2 x NLSE diesels / 2 x
	electric motors
Range	Not known

On the other hand, submarines now faced more effective anti-submarine weapons. The depth charge was not invented until the middle of World War I, but by 1939 it was a mature technology which could be dropped from aircraft as well as surface vessels. Aircraft could also attack with bombs or rockets, and now had sufficient range to threaten submarines that were far from land.

Aircraft Threat

Aircraft speeds had also vastly increased, and this reduced the time available to dive and escape. Many later submarines had two alarm systems controlled from the conning tower. One instructed the crew to crash-dive with all haste. The other was an instruction to man anti-aircraft weapons to defend the boat. Choosing which to use was a critical decision – a submarine caught mid-dive with its stern in the air was extremely vulnerable to air attack. So although the submarines of World War II (1939–1945) were much more advanced than their predecessors, they faced much more effective countermeasures.

ABOVE: The French *Surcouf* was built as a 'submarine cruiser' for commerce raiding.

LEFT: The addition of radar enabled submarines to locate targets from beyond visual range and, perhaps more importantly, receive warning of hostile aircraft in time to dive.

Axis Submarines of Early World War II

Germany started the war

with an inadequate fleet of 38 ocean-capable U-boats, and emphasis was at first placed on surface warship construction, rather than rapid expansion of this force. Nevertheless, with the almost immediate imposition of unrestricted submarine warfare, these boats caused serious losses to Allied merchant shipping.

The Allies tried, unsuccessfully, to counter the U-boats by aggressive measures – patrolling areas the boats had to pass through in order to get to and from their home ports. This suited the aggressive mentality of naval officers but did not achieve much. Indeed, the loss of an aircraft carrier to torpedo attack while carrying out anti-submarine sweeps demonstrated the dangers inherent in this policy. The U-boats had an advantage they had lacked in World War I. The conquest of France gave access

to bases on the French coast. This meant that the U-boats had easy access to the Atlantic and the western approaches to Britain without having to sail right around Britain or through the heavily patrolled English Channel.

Milk Cows

The period up to December 1941 was referred to as the 'happy time' by the U-boat service. The countermeasures in place were not sufficient to prevent the majority of attacks and as a result the submarines ran wild, sinking huge tonnages of merchant ships. The typical early-war U-boat was a Type VII, capable of operating 200m (656ft) down and making 8 knots submerged. Armed with five 533mm (21in) torpedo tubes, an 88mm (3.5in) deck gun and a 20mm (.79in) anti-aircraft gun, the Type VII was extremely effective. Patrols were extended by resupply from transport submarines known as 'milk cows'. Later in the war these large subs suffered unacceptable casualties and were withdrawn.

Italy contributed over 100 submarines to the war in the Mediterranean. Many

ABOVE: *U-47* successfully penetrated the Royal Navy base at Scapa Flow and torpedoed the battleship HMS *Royal Oak*.

BELOW: Successful U-boat crews were often used as propaganda heroes. The crew of *U-47* were perhaps the most famous of all.

were of modern and capable designs. The *Brin* class mounted four 533mm (21in) torpedo tubes fore and the same aft, with 6 reload torpedoes, plus a 120mm (4.7in) deck gun. The Imperial Japanese Navy viewed its submarines as an adjunct to the battle fleet, operating them in squadrons as reconnaissance assets rather than as raiders. This neglect of the commerce raider role carried over into defensive thinking – the Japanese suffered heavily from submarine attacks on their merchant marine and fleet train assets.

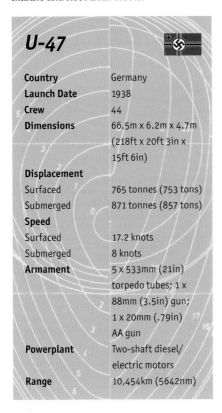

U-47

Country	Germany
Launch Date	1938
Crew	44
Dimensions	66.5m x 6.2m x 4.7m (218ft x 20ft 3in x 15ft 6in)
Displacement	
Surfaced	765 tonnes (753 tons)
Submerged	871 tonnes (857 tons)
Speed	
Surfaced	17.2 knots
Submerged	8 knots
Armament	5 x 533mm (21in) torpedo tubes; 1 x 88mm (3.5in) gun; 1 x 20mm (.79in) AA gun
Powerplant	Two-shaft diesel/ electric motors
Range	10,454km (5642nm)

U-47 was a Type VIIC U-boat, the mainstay of the German submarine war.

The VIIC class mounted a deck gun for surface attacks, along with 14 torpedoes fired from four bow and one stern torpedo tubes.

ABOVE: *U-47* carried out 10 war patrols, sinking 32 vessels over the period of 238 days at sea. She was finally sunk, probably by two Royal Navy corvettes, in March 1941.

The hull of the *U-47* was tough enough to withstand depth-charging for extended periods.

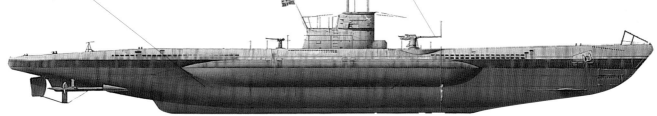

Allied Submarines of Early World War II

Many British boats of the early war were roughly equivalent in size to the Type VII U-boats. The 'S' class, dating from the early 1930s, displaced 650 tons on the surface and carried six 533mm (21in) torpedo tubes.

The boats intended for fleet operations (in conjunction with the surface fleet) needed to be faster on the surface and tended to be larger. The 21-knot *Thames* class displaced 1834 tonnes (1805 tons) but did not carry significantly heavier armament to the 'S' class. The French submarine fleet did not have much opportunity to contribute to the war, though Free French forces did operate a number of boats after the surrender of their government.

US Developments

The US Navy did not pursue submarine construction or development very vigorously in the inter-war years, but greatly increased production at the start of the 1940s. The *Gato* class, with six bow and four stern torpedo tubes, was the standard US fleet submarine at the outset of the war. The *Gatos* and subsequent classes derived from them were large – about twice the size of an Atlantic-capable U-boat.

US submarines needed to operate over very long distances in the Pacific theatre. They were hampered early in the war by an extremely cautious doctrine and defective torpedoes. Far more torpedoes malfunctioned than exploded even when a hit was made, and ammunition stocks were low. Submarine captains were urged to conserve ammunition rather than taking any opportunity for an attack.

This policy gradually changed, and at the same time more and better torpedoes became available. Increased aggression and weapons that actually worked resulted in an extremely effective campaign against Japanese shipping as the war continued. The USA did not enter the war until 1941, and the submarine campaign did not get going for some time afterwards. Nevertheless, by the end of the war the US submarine service had succeeded in crippling the Japanese merchant fleet. This cut the home islands off from vital raw materials and greatly reduced Japanese warfighting capability in the long term.

ABOVE: The 'S' class was designed to meet a Royal Navy requirement for smaller boats which were well suited to the North Sea and Mediterranean.

BELOW: The US *Gato* class was built in large numbers and served as the basis for the later *Balao* and *Tench* classes.

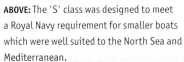

USS *Gato*

Country	USA
Launch Date	1941
Crew	
Dimensions	95.02m x 8.31m x 5.18m (311ft 9in x 27ft 3in x 17ft)
Displacement	
Surfaced	1549 tonnes (1525 tons)
Submerged	8334 tonnes (2386 tons)
Speed	
Surfaced	21 knots
Submerged	9 knots
Armament	10 × 21 in (533 mm) torpedo tubes, 24 torpedoes; 1 x 102mm (4in)/50 calibre deck gun; four MGs
Powerplant	4 × GM Model 16-248 V16 diesel engines, 4 × high-speed GE electric motors
Range	20,372km (11,000 nm)

Axis Submarines Of Late World War II

Most nations suffered

problems with their torpedoes early in the war. Some defects were avoidable – such as depth settings based on practice warheads that did not weigh the same as live weapons, so ran deeper than expected. This could cause a torpedo to pass beneath a vessel on the surface without detonating.

Wolf Packs

Other problems with torpedoes were technical – many simply failed to explode because their detonators were defective. Better torpedoes were accompanied by advances in submarine design and construction and successful wolf-pack tactics. This idea was implemented as early as 1940 and was used throughout the war. By cooperating, a team of U–boats could ensure that at least one boat was in position to make an attack. Shifting patrol areas also paid dividends – a handful of boats operating off Florida in 1942 caused severe losses to American shipping which was silhouetted against the lights of the shore.

The grim Battle of the Atlantic began in earnest in 1942, but already the tide was turning. Aircraft, using rockets, bombs and depth charges, took an increasing toll among U-boats, especially as they transited the Bay of Biscay en route to, and from, their bases. To counter this, some boats gained increased anti-aircraft armament. Their captains had a choice between crash-diving and staying on the surface to fight it out. Another way of reducing submarine losses was to avoid surfacing, using a 'snorkel' to obtain air for the crew and engines while the boat remained submerged. This was imperfect but it did help the U-boats maintain their primary advantage of stealth.

Hitler's New Design

In an attempt to tip the balance back in favour of his U-boats, Hitler decided to proceed with the construction of hydrogen peroxide-powered boats. These had been demonstrated some

LEFT: Hydrography developed hand-in-hand with submarine design. Accurate plotting of water conditions was of immense benefit to German U-boat commanders.

time previously but at that point it seemed that conventional boats were entirely sufficient. The new boat, designated Type XVIII, was obviously not going to be ready in time to make a difference so a more conventional diesel-electric U-boat was based on the design. This became the Type XXI. It used the large space intended for hydrogen peroxide storage to house extra batteries, giving increased underwater range and performance. After the war, the British experimented with hydrogen peroxide- powered boats derived from wartime German experiments. They proved to be extremely hazardous to operate.

ABOVE: The Type XXI U-boat had a greatly increased battery capacity, enabling it to travel submerged for 2–3 days at a time.

LEFT: The schnorkel concept was in common use from 1944 onwards, enabling boats to run their diesel engines whilst remaining submerged.

Type XXI

Country	Germany
Launch Date	1944
Crew	57
Dimensions	77m x 8m x 6.2m (251ft 8in x 26ft 3in x 20ft 4in)
Displacement	
Surfaced	1647 tonnes (1621 tons)
Submerged	2100 tonnes (2067 tons)
Speed	
Surfaced	15.5 knots
Submerged	16 knots
Armament	6 x 533mm (21in) torpedo tubes; 4 x 30mm (1.2in) AA guns
Powerplant	Twin screws, diesel/ electric motors, silent creeping motors
Range	9684km (9678nm)

The Type XXI U-boat was double hulled. The outer hull was light and streamlined and the inner hull was made of high-carbon steel.

In addition to her main engines, the Type XXI could run silently at 3.5 knots underwater using 'creeper' engines.

The Type XXI's submerged speed was actually greater than when surfaced.

Allied Submarines of Late World War II

As the war continued, the US overcame problems with its weapons and adopted a far more aggressive stance. It was not uncommon for US submarines to duel with the escorts in the hope of eliminating them and gaining an opportunity to wipe out a convoy, rather than torpedoing a single ship and making off.

The Japanese Navy never really appreciated the need for anti-submarine vessels or techniques. Right to the end of the war, merchant ships sailed alone or in very lightly escorted convoys. As a result over 1000 Japanese ships were sunk by US submarines, including a battleship and eight aircraft carriers. US submarines also undertook a range of special duties, including carrying fuel to resupply long-range seaplanes and landing forces on enemy-held islands.

Stalin's Soviet Subs

The Russian submarine fleet was the largest of all the Allies, but played relatively little part in the war. This was largely due to Stalin's purges in the years before the war. Otherwise excellent officers were dismissed or imprisoned on the slightest suspicion of political unreliability, leaving their jobs open to more politically-minded but less competent men, or sometimes just junior ranks over-promoted to fill the vacuum. As a result, the Russian submarine service was poorly led and inefficient. However, Soviet boats were active in the Baltic throughout the war. Although many boats were more involved with minelaying operations rather than direct attacks, Russian submarines constantly threatened the movements of war material and reinforcements in the Baltic.

Bigger and Quieter

Britain built considerable numbers of submarines during the war years, usually in large classes such as the 'S' and 'U' class. Operational experience led to a number of design changes as the war went on. Later models of the 'U' class gained a longer hull which altered the flow of water over the propellers, making the boat quieter. Towards the end of the war the Royal Navy began building large submarines intended for operations in the Pacific against the Japanese. These boats incorporated the capability to lay mines and had external torpedo tubes in addition to their reloadable internal ones. Wartime experience resulted in these boats being quieter and faster to dive than previous classes.

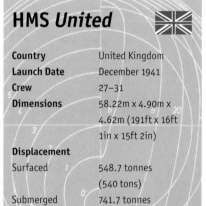

HMS *United*

Country	United Kingdom
Launch Date	December 1941
Crew	27–31
Dimensions	58.22m x 4.90m x 4.62m (191ft x 16ft 1in x 15ft 2in)
Displacement	
Surfaced	548.7 tonnes (540 tons)
Submerged	741.7 tonnes (730 tons)
Speed	
Surfaced	11.25 knots
Submerged	10 knots
Armament	4 x 533mm (21in) torpedo tubes; 8–10 torpedoes; 1 x 76.2mm (3in) gun
Powerplant	2 x shaft diesel-electric; 2 x 615kW (825hp) Paxman Ricardo diesel generators + electric
Range	Not known

ABOVE: A submarine's conning tower raised a lookout a little above sea level, increasing its visual range. Constant vigilance allowed a submarine to escape danger by diving.

BELOW: 51 boats of the 'U' class were built for the Royal Navy. Although effective in combat, these vessels suffered heavy losses.

Special Operations Boats in World War II

Ordinary submarines were

pressed into service for unorthodox jobs at times. Submarines brought supplies into Malta when surface vessels could not get through, and delivered reconnaissance teams or raiding forces into enemy territory.

Submarines were sometimes fitted with beacon lights to guide amphibious forces ashore and even rocket batteries for bombardment purposes. Such tasks were within the capabilities of any submarine, but some boats were specially designed for unusual operations. Among them were the British X-craft, small submarines designed to sneak into enemy harbours and plant charges under major ships such as the battleship Tirpitz. These were in no way suicide craft, though their mission was certainly hazardous.

Torpedo Divers

Human torpedoes were used by several combatants, but none (other than the Japanese) considered them to be suicide weapons. Instead they were a means to get a diver and an explosive charge close to an enemy warship at anchor, at which point he could set the timer and attempt to withdraw.

The Japanese did deploy suicide craft in the form of Kaiten torpedoes. These were converted Long Lance torpedoes guided to the target by a crewman. They sank a handful of Allied ships. However, underwater weapons of this type are not well suited to the Kamikaze mentality. Sneaking through harbour defences requires a calculating sort of courage that is different from the reckless frame of mind needed to crash a speeding aircraft onto a target.

Seaplane Subs

On a rather more grand scale, the Japanese Navy built several

X-5	🇬🇧
Country	United Kingdom
Launch Date	1942
Crew	4
Dimensions	15.7m x 1.8m x 2.6m (51ft 6in x 6ft x 8ft 6in)
Displacement	
Surfaced	27.4 tonnes (27 tons)
Submerged	29.97 tonnes (29.5 tons)
Speed	
Surfaced	6.5 knots
Submerged	5 knots
Armament	Explosive charges
Powerplant	Single screw, diesel/ electric motors
Range	Not recorded

RIGHT: British X-Craft midget submarines were towed close to the target before being boarded by the crew for the final approach.

seaplane- carrying submarines. Some were fleet boats equipped with an aircraft for reconnaissance, but others were intended for strike missions. The giant *I-400* class was built to carry four seaplanes. It was planned to attack the Panama Canal with these vessels, but the war ended while they were en route. Aircraft-carrying submarines were extremely inefficient, and the resources poured into the *I-400* class seem to have been entirely wasted. Certainly, although the idea has been kicked around from time to time, no navy has attempted to build an aircraft-carrying submarine since the end of the war.

ABOVE: The Imperial Japanese Navy made a serious effort at creating a submarine-aircraft-carrier in the *I-400* class. These huge and expensive boats never made any contribution to the war.

RIGHT: The Kaiten manned torpedo was a theoretically sound weapon, given the willingness of crewmen to make a suicide attack, but it did not achieve much success.

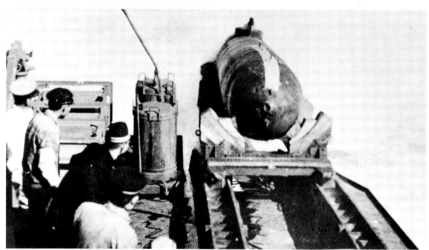

The *I-400* class carried three assembled Seiran floatplanes and a fourth as components.

After warming up the engine in the hangar, the aircraft was placed in the launching position unfolded.

Launch was assisted by a 26m (85ft) catapult over the bow. For recovery, aircraft landed on the sea and were lifted aboard by crane.

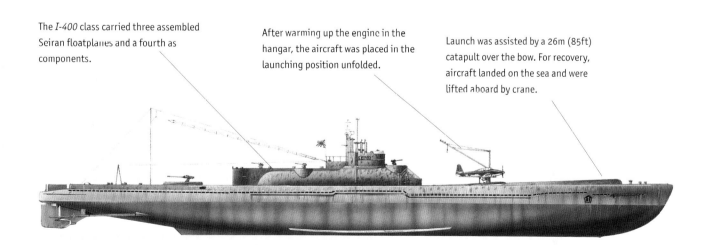

Post-War to the Present Day

Propulsion Systems

In 1939, scientists suggested that a submarine could be powered by nuclear energy, giving it virtually unlimited range. This did not come to pass for some years, but in the meantime various experiments were undertaken into better propulsion systems for submarines.

The main problem was getting engines to function without needing an outside air supply. Hydrogen peroxide offered a possible solution, releasing large quantities of energy without consuming air. Experimental German boats using this system had been successfully trialled but were expensive to run.

Hydrogen Peroxide Power

The British obtained examples of hydrogen peroxide-powered boats, which could top 25 knots submerged, and began their own experiments. The vessels chosen were *Excalibur* and *Explorer*, custom-built submarines with streamlined hulls. These two boats proved the concept was viable but suffered so many accidents that they became known in naval circles as 'Excruciator' and 'Exploder' respectively. The advent of nuclear power removed the need for dangerous and expensive hydrogen peroxide-powered boats. The main contribution of *Explorer* and *Excalibur* was in the field of hull development. Previous boats normally used a hull configuration designed for surface running. Such vessels needed a keel to increase stability and were streamlined in a similar manner to surface ships. Post-war submarines were more geared to underwater running and gradually moved towards the modern cylindrical hull which fully submerges underwater.

Worldwide Catch-up

Other nations also began to obtain submarine forces, often by buying surplus war-built boats from the Allies. This greatly increased the possibility that a small-scale conflict might involve submarine forces, and consequently forced many navies into increasing

their anti-submarine capabilities. There have been very few actions involving submarines in the post-war world. During the Cold War there were numerous alleged incursions by Soviet boats into Swedish waters, and the Swedes made several attacks on what they claimed were Soviet subs. The details of these incidents remain unclear in many cases.

Submarines played an important part in the Falklands conflict of 1982. The Argentine Navy possessed a small submarine force which attempted to penetrate the defences of the British task force, without success. British submarines were rather more influential, though there was only one sinking. In the Cold War, the Warsaw Pact and NATO tested their submarines and anti-submarine forces against one another, attempting to penetrate

defences to gather information, and harassing one another's boats. To some extent, this harassment was a useful deterrent as it demonstrated to the potential enemy that his boats could be found and sunk if necessary.

ABOVE: HMS *Explorer*, one of two experimental submarines, was nicknamed 'Exploder' as a consequence of her many accidents.

BELOW: HMS *Excalibur*, sister to *Explorer*, was nicknamed 'Excruciator' for similar reasons. Important lessons concerning hull design were learned from these boats.

HMS *Excalibur*

Country	United Kingdom
Launch Date	1955
Crew	49
Dimensions	54m x 4.8m x 3.4m (178ft x 15ft 8in x 11ft)
Displacement	
Surfaced	780 tonnes (767 tons)
Submerged	1000 tonnes (984 tons)
Speed	
Submerged	25 knots
Armament	None
Powerplant	High Test Peroxide (HTP) steam-raising plant driving steam turbines (submerged); diesel-electric (surfaced)
Range	Not known

Western Attack Subs of the Early Cold War

In the immediate post-war period, wartime designs soldiered on for a while, but gradually modern attack submarines emerged. The role of an attack submarine is to sink enemy surface ships and submarines, ideally by surprise attack. Advances were made in weaponry and sensors, while boats were made as quiet as possible.

Nuclear Power

Most nations continued to use diesel-electric boats, albeit of increasingly advanced design. Those nations that chose to pursue nuclear-powered submarines took a gamble. The development process was expensive and fraught with difficulties. Once nuclear boats were available, however, their high sustained speeds and immense endurance allowed operations anywhere in the world. Nuclear boats are to some extent a return to steam power. The reactor is used to heat water to make steam, which drives a turbine that in turn generates electricity to power the boat and run the motors. There is a bank of batteries for emergency use. In many cases, submarines returned to their early role of coastal defence. One example is the Italian *Enrico Toti* class, a small boat designed for the shallow waters of the Mediterranean Sea. These boats were designed to lurk at choke points where geography forced ships through a narrow channel, conducting an ambush, then sneaking away to find a new target.

Built to Endure

Some nations implemented a mix of diesel boats for shorter range operations and nuclear attack subs for long patrols worldwide. Nuclear boats are actually more noisy than diesel submarines as they have to keep the reactor pumps running where a diesel-electric boat running on batteries is all but silent. However, the endurance advantage of nuclear boats offsets this factor in the eyes of many navies. In the West, greater emphasis began to be placed on hunting and sinking enemy submarines rather than surface vessels. This largely came about as a result of the threat posed by the vastly expanded Soviet submarine fleet, which seriously threatened Western merchant shipping in the event of a war.

BELOW: USS *Skate* set a number of impressive 'firsts', including first transit under the North Pole and the first entirely submerged crossing of the Atlantic.

A small-sized hull minimizes sonar cross-section and makes the boat hard to detect.

Lack of deck guns improves underwater performance and quietness.

Four 533mm (21in) torpedo tubes can launch guided torpedoes against surface or underwater targets.

ABOVE: The Italian *Enrico Toti* class submarine, entering service in 1967, was designed as a small coastal vessel optimized for the shallow, cluttered waters off Italy.

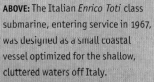

USS *Skate*

Country	USA
Launch Date	1955
Crew	8 officers and 76 men
Dimensions	7.6m x 81.56m (267ft 7in x 25ft)
Displacement	
Surfaced	2590 tonnes (2550 tons)
Submerged	2894 tonnes (2848 tons)
Speed	
Surfaced	15.5 knots
Armament	8 × 533mm (21in) torpedo tubes (6 forward, 2 aft)
Powerplant	1 x S3W nuclear reactor
Range	Unlimited

Warsaw Pact Attack Subs of the Early Cold War

In the West, emphasis was increasingly placed on aircraft carriers for both land attack and operations against surface shipping. The Soviet Union, being primarily a land power, was less concerned with naval power projection but needed a counter to the carrier battle groups.

The Soviet Union needed a means to prevent reinforcement of Europe in the event that the Cold War became 'hot'. In addition to a powerful surface fleet, the Soviet Union and its allies in the Warsaw Pact began constructing large numbers of submarines. These were more geared to sinking surface ships than attacking submarines. Large numbers of diesel-electric boats were laid down. These could undertake long ocean patrols but were also used for defensive purposes.

Nuclear attack boats became available from 1958, four years after the US Navy launched the world's first nuclear-powered submarine, fittingly named *Nautilus*. The 'November' class were the first Soviet nuclear boats, capable of 30 knots underwater and armed with nuclear torpedoes that could devastate a carrier battle group with a near miss. These boats were noisy and thus easy to track and in addition were prone to serious problems with their powerplants.

Cat and Mouse

More advanced boats followed, and a naval arms race ensued between the Warsaw Pact and NATO as each sought to build faster, quieter, or more potently armed vessels and to counter those of the opposition with better sensors and fire control systems. To a great extent the Cold War was fought underwater, as attack subs of both sides played a dangerous game of cat-and-mouse, harassing one another while gaining data on the capabilities of the opposition.

The advent of nuclear power enabled submarines to operate under the arctic ice cap, which presented a whole new array of challenges. The underside of pack ice is not uniform, and thick ridges of ice can project down as much as 50m (164ft). Icebergs can go much deeper; sometimes as much as 400m (1312ft). Navigating in such an environment is a considerable challenge and specialist ice-detecting SONAR systems have been developed to help.

USS *Nautilus*

Country	USA
Launch Date	1954
Crew	105
Dimensions	97m x 8.4m x 6.6m (323ft 7in x 27ft 8in x 21ft 9in)
Displacement	
Surfaced	4157 tonnes (4091 tons)
Submerged	4104 tonnes (4040 tons)
Speed	
Surfaced	20 knots
Submerged	23 knots
Armament	6 x 533mm (21in) torpedo tubes
Powerplant	Twin screws, one S2W reactor, turbines
Range	Unlimited

Nautilus featured a modern fin rather than the traditional conning tower of wartime and previous boats.

Nautilus had an armament of six 533mm (21in) torpedo tubes in the bow.

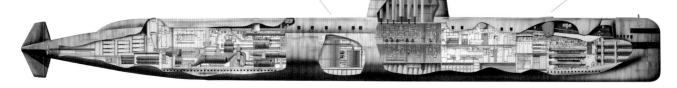

ABOVE: The 'November' class was the Soviet Union's first nuclear-powered submarine. It was designed to sink surface ships.

LEFT: USS *Nautilus* set new records including a transit of over 2000km (1080nm) in 90 hours without surfacing.

Early Missile Boats to Modern Boomers

In 1942, a German U-boat successfully launched a salvo of artillery rockets from 15m (49ft) below the surface, prompting interest in missile-launching submarines. A plan to use a nuclear-tipped V2 rocket launched by a submarine against New York was drawn up, but this project was overtaken by events and never completed.

After the war, NATO and the Warsaw Pact developed the idea further. Early attempts were clumsy and only marginally effective – USS *Grayback* was capable of launching two Regulus missiles with a range of 804km (434nm). This required approaching close to a hostile coast and launching from the surface, virtually ensuring that the submarine would not escape retribution. Improvements followed quickly, with the introduction of vessels capable of carrying several missiles and launching while underwater. It has become standard practice for ballistic missiles to be carried upright in launch tubes mounted vertically in the submarine either forward or aft of the sail.

Long Range Attack

As missile range and accuracy increased, it became possible to attack an enemy's cities from halfway around the world. This meant that missile boats no longer needed to approach an enemy coast to launch their weapons. They could hide anywhere in the oceans and strike by surprise. The main advantage of submarine-launched missiles is that they are hard to eliminate with a first strike, and thus make an excellent deterrent as retaliation is certain. However, the subs must be protected from attack. Most Western powers do this by hiding them in nondescript areas of ocean; most of the crew do not know where their patrol area is, so security is easy to maintain.

Precision Strikes

The Warsaw Pact developed a strategy of creating 'bastions' – sea areas bounded

USS *Grayback*

Country	USA
Launch Date	1957
Crew	87
Dimensions	83m x 8.28m x 5.8m (273ft x 27ft 2in x 19ft)
Displacement	2812 tonnes (2768 tons)
Speed	14 knots
Armament	8 × torpedo tubes, 1 × Regulus missile launcher
Powerplant	Not known
Range	Not known

by land on some sides and heavily defended by attack subs, aircraft, minefields and surface vessels. Some boats are capable of launching cruise missiles rather than strategic ballistic weapons. Some of these weapons, such as the Tomahawk missile, can carry a nuclear warhead but can also be used in a more conventional role for precision strikes on important targets. Thus the missile submarine has now become capable of land attack, a role traditionally performed by surface craft armed with large guns.

ABOVE: US *Halibut* was the first submarine designed to launch missiles. Her later career was spent as a special operations sub involved in espionage missions.

RIGHT: The first submarine-launched missiles were codenamed Regulus.

BELOW: USS *Grayback* was intended to be an attack submarine but was converted to launch Regulus missiles.

Advanced Soviet Attack Subs

In order to attack Western carrier battle groups more effectively and to counter increasingly advanced anti-submarine warfare (ASW) capabilities, the Warsaw Pact developed ever more potent attack submarines.

In the 1970s, the 'Alfa' class appeared. This was a large and extremely fast nuclear attack boat, capable of 42 knots underwater and armed with a mix of nuclear and conventional torpedoes. At the time, it was thought that the 'Alfa's' could dive deep enough to evade all available torpedoes, prompting research into deep-running torpedoes that proved unnecessary. Like many such threats, it turned out that the 'Alfa' was not so potent as it seemed –

the reactors were very unreliable and maximum depth was nothing like so deep as first feared.

Reliable Diesel

Not all advanced attack boats were nuclear-powered, however. The 'Kilo' class, which appeared in the 1980s, is diesel-powered yet capable of 24 knots underwater. These boats have met with considerable export success, granting modern attack-boat capabilities to navies that could not afford to develop their own vessels.

Before the Soviet Union broke up, very advanced boats were beginning to appear. These included the 'Sierra' class, which has been reported as

The hull was not designed for deep diving as was assumed in the West, but is capable of reaching a test depth of 350m (1148ft).

The 'Alfa' class had a liquid-metal reactor capable of driving the boat at 42 knots underwater.

The 'Alfa' class featured six torpedo tubes capable of launching conventional or nuclear torpedoes.

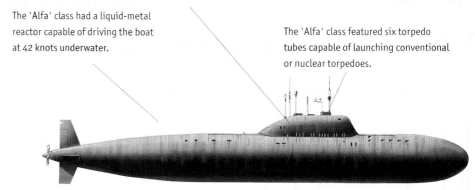

LEFT: The 'Akula' class attack submarine can use torpedoes against ships or submarines, and missiles to attack surface targets and coastal installations.

ABOVE: The 'Sierra' class was designed for high underwater speed and stealth, with a large gap between the pressure hull and outer casing to reduce noise.

BOTTOM: The 'Alfa' class caused grave consternation in the West due to its assumed deep-diving capabilities.

'Alfa' Class

Country	USSR
Launch Date	1970
Crew	31
Dimensions	81m x 9.5m x 8m (265ft 9in x 31ft 2in x 26ft 3in)
Displacement	
Surfaced	2845 tonnes (2899 tons)
Submerged	3739 tonnes (3680 tons)
Speed	14 knots
Surfaced	20 knots
Submerged	42 knots
Armament	6 x 533mm (21in) torpedo tubes; torpedoes; 36 mines
Powerplant	Liquid-metal reactor, two steam turbines
Range	Unlimited

successfully testing at a depth of 1000m (3280ft), and the cheaper 'Akula' class. Lack of funds precluded development of new boats for many years, but the improved circumstances of the former Soviet states may finally permit new classes of attack submarine to be considered. As these more advanced boats became available, older subs were sold on to friendly governments. Significant numbers of 'Whiskey' and 'Romeo' class boats in particular were sold overseas. In some cases these vessels were used to gain experience with submarines and a head-start in

the design stakes by nations wanting to create a powerful submarine force but which did not want to start at the bottom of the learning curve.

The Soviet Union was successful to a great extent in concealing the capabilities of its boats. This forced NATO analysts to guess at what any given vessel was capable of. The distinctive pod mounted at the stern of the 'Sierra' and 'Akula' class attack subs caused great consternation, for example. Theories about its function ranged from housing an advanced sensor array to some kind of new propulsion system.

Advanced Western Attack Subs

The evolution of the attack submarine continued throughout the Cold War period and afterwards, though sometimes in fits and starts. World events and advancing foreign capabilities prompted new initiatives.

The *Los Angeles* class attack submarine came about largely as a result of the realization that a US carrier group could not outrun a Soviet 'November' class attack boat. The capabilities of the modern attack submarine were demonstrated in 1982 when a British nuclear sub, HMS *Conqueror*, torpedoed and sank the Argentinian cruiser *General Belgrano* during the Falklands War. The Argentine navy was large and powerful, but was so intimidated by the threat of one or more nuclear boats outside its ports (in fact *Conqueror* was alone at that point) that it did not come out to fight.

Large and Small

The last Cold War era attack sub to come into service was the *Seawolf* class, which was designed in 1982. Large, fast, quiet and enormously capable, *Seawolf* was designed to counter the best the Warsaw Pact could field, but entered service too late to play a part in the Cold War. The smallest class of nuclear attack submarine is the *Rubis* class built for the French navy. These boats date from the late 1970s, but have all been updated to the standards of the last-built boats, incorporating new technologies to create the *Rubis/Amethyste* class. Displacement is 2670 tonnes (2627 tons) submerged, about equivalent to a *Thames* class fleet submarine of the 1930s and much larger than the typical wartime U-boat. The British *Astute* class attack submarine is enormous by the standards of World War II boats, displacing some 7400 tons submerged. It is hard to describe a vessel of this size, which is equivalent to a destroyer or cruiser, as a 'boat', but the tradition endures.

Big boats are necessary to transport all the equipment and personnel required to carry out their role, or more accurately, roles. Today's Western attack subs are likely to have to function in a variety of environments, including operating in shallow coastal waters. Since the 1991 Gulf War, attack submarines have conducted land attacks with missiles, and many boats can also launch missiles against enemy surface ships.

HMS *Astute*

Country	United Kingdom
Launch Date	2007
Crew	98
Dimensions	87m x 11.3m x 10m
	(323ft x 37ft x 33ft)
Displacement	
Surfaced	7000 tonnes (6889 tons)
Submerged	7400 tonnes (7137 tons)
Speed	
Submerged	29 knots
Armament	6 x 533mm (21in) torpedo tubes, 38 Spearfish torpedoes, UGM-84 Harpoon and Tomahawk Block IV cruise missiles, naval mines
Powerplant	Rolls-Royce PWR2 reactor, MTU diesel generators
Range	Circumnavigation 40 times without refuelling

ABOVE: The *Los Angeles* class nuclear-powered attack submarine can launch cruise missiles from its torpedo tubes.

BELOW: The keel of HMS *Astute*, a nuclear-powered attack submarine, was laid down exactly a century from the date work began on the first Royal Navy submarine.

Chinese Military Submarines

Most of China's early

Submarines came from the Soviet Union, including 'Romeo' class attack boats and plans for a 'Golf' class missile sub. However, cooling relations between China and the Soviet Union forced the Chinese to go it alone. China built a developed version of the 'Romeo' class, which was capable of minelaying or undertaking a rather basic attack sub role. The first Chinese nuclear attack boat was the 'Han' class, built with German assistance. The Chinese settled for lower capabilities than other navies, perhaps seeing the 'Han' class as a learning experience. Despite their relative simplicity these boats are considered unreliable and accident-prone.

Gaining Experience

The 'Xia' class missile submarine was developed from the 'Han' class and it, too, has had problems along the way. This is not uncommon with first-generation weapon systems, which the 'Xia' is, to a great extent. Although China entered the submarine warfare stakes late and benefited somewhat from the experiences of others, there is no substitute for first-hand experience.

Second-generation boats are now entering service. The 'Shang' class attack boats are perhaps a generation behind US attack submarines in terms of quietness and capability, but the Chinese navy is gaining experience that will permit the eventual development of world-class vessels.

'Kilo' Class

China also obtained a number of 'Kilo' class diesel-electric boats from Russia. The 'Kilo' has been a considerable export success and may eventually form the basis of other classes developed overseas by purchasers. The 'Kilo' class has a teardrop-shaped hull form which has more in common with Western boats than Russian designs. It is entirely likely that this will influence future Chinese submarine development.

Aspirational Fleet

Submarines are an important part of any modern navy, and China's interests in the Pacific seem to require an expanded fleet, so more submarines are likely to appear. It is not possible to enforce overseas territorial claims without a credible fleet, for example, and China's claim to the Spratly Islands is more likely to be upheld if backed by a modern 'blue-water' navy. In any case, a powerful navy is seen as a status symbol and a deterrent against aggression by most powers, making continued naval expansion desirable if China's capabilities are to keep pace with her aspirations.

BELOW: The Chinese Navy's first nuclear-powered submarines were the 'Han' class, introduced in the 1970s.

'Kilo' Class

Country	China
Launch Date	1980
Crew	45–50
Dimensions	69m x 9m x 7m (226ft 5in x 29ft 6in x 23ft)
Displacement	
Surfaced	2494 tonnes (2454 tons)
Submerged	3103 tonnes (3053 tons)
Speed	
Submerged	24 knots
Armament	Six 533mm (21in) torpedo tubes
Powerplant	Single shaft, three diesels, three electric motors
Range	11,112km (6000nm)

TOP: 'Kilo' class submarines can be easily identified by their tear-shaped hull.

LEFT: Of China's two 'Xia' class ballistic missile submarines, one is reported as having been lost due to an unspecified accident.

Special Operations Boats

Submarines are able to operate in areas a surface craft would be unable to enter, enabling them to carry out special operations or to gather intelligence about foreign vessels, seabed conditions, shore installations and so forth.

Some of these missions can be carried out by any boat, though as a rule small diesel-electric subs are better suited to covert coastal operations than large ocean-going nuclear attack boats. Some missions require a converted or custom-built vessel.

Special Operations

A submarine can act as a mobile listening post by riding at periscope depth with its antennae deployed and collecting enemy emissions. Much can be learned from the types of radar emitting in a given area even if communications cannot be intercepted and decoded. Some boats are able to deliver special forces teams. One conversion that has been used for this purpose was shelters on the deck of the submarine, in which special forces divers could ride as they approached the target, swimming out to fulfill their mission. Some special operations subs have airlocks to permit divers to enter and exit the craft, carrying out sabotage or reconnaissance missions in hostile waters while the submarine waits nearby.

Small Saboteurs

Bottom-crawling submarines have also been considered for covert infiltration missions, either delivering teams to the land or conducting a covert mission in an enemy anchorage. None

of these roles really needs a full-scale submarine. Small special operations boats are easier to handle in coastal conditions and shallow water and are also cheaper to operate, freeing the attack subs for more mainstream warfighting roles.

These small boats can be carried to their operational areas aboard larger vessels. For example, the Russian 'India' class submarine can carry special operations boats in place of her Deep Submergence Rescue Vehicles, delivering them to the target area and enabling them to make a speedy withdrawal after the mission.

The 'Sea Dagger' submarine is a modular design which can be tailored to a range of activities by inserting the correct mission-specific module. It can function as a short-range attack boat or a swimmer delivery vehicle, reconnaissance platform or training unit to assist in the development of anti-submarine techniques. At present, 'Sea Dagger' is the only vessel of its type, but it is possible that more mission-configurable craft will become available in future.

ABOVE: The 'India' class was designed for salvage and rescue operations but can also deliver special operations troops.

LEFT: US Navy SEAL teams are trained to conduct demolitions and other special tasks underwater.

'India' Class

Country	Russia
Launch Date	1979
Crew	70
Dimensions	106m x 10m (347ft 9in x 32ft 8in)
Displacement	
Surfaced	3251 tonnes (3200 tons)
Submerged	4064 tonnes (4000 tons)
Speed	
Submerged	10 knots
Surfaced	15 knots
Armament	4 x 533mm (21in) torpedo tubes
Powerplant	Twin screws, diesel/ electric motors
Range	Not known

Modern Multi-role Submarines

The majority of navies cannot afford to develop their own first-line attack submarines – indeed, few can afford to operate them even if they are purchased overseas. However, a submarine capability is an effective deterrent and is often seen as desirable.

Surplus Vessels

One solution is to buy surplus vessels from navies which are upgrading to newer designs, but such boats are usually well past their best. A range of vessels are available for export which provide attack-sub capability at a fairly modest price. Boats of this type are mainly used for coastal patrols and defence of offshore assets, but can fulfil most warfighting roles. Although lower in capability than a cutting-edge nuclear attack boat, they are equipped with modern sensors and fire-control electronics, creating a vessel that is vastly more capable than a second or third-hand surplus boat.

BELOW: Despite some technical problems, the *Collins* class is a highly effective diesel-electric attack boat built for the Royal Australian Navy.

German-designed submarines are in service with various nations, sometimes in modernized or modified form. The boats are offered in a range of configurations, allowing them to be tailored to the needs of the end user.

Types 206 and 209

The Type 206, which achieved considerable export success, was developed from a Cold War-era diesel attack boat intended for operations in the restricted waters of the Baltic. It was small and manoeuvrable, and these characteristics were inherited by its successor. Type 206s are gradually disappearing as they are replaced by more modern boats. In German service their replacement is the Type 212A. An export version with sensitive technologies

replaced with more conventional systems, is now offered for export.

The larger Type 209 submarine has also been a big export success. Some versions can launch the submarine version of the Harpoon anti-ship missile; others mount only torpedoes. The Type 209 can be configured in various ways indicated by a second number after a slash, such as Type 209/1400. This indicates the submerged displacement of the vessel and gives a general indication of what systems are fitted.

RIGHT: The Type 206 is a successful modern diesel-electric design used by Germany and Israel. They can carry up to 24 mines externally.

BELOW: Designed in Germany with the export market in mind, the Type 209 design was based on the Type 206.

Schnorkel apparatus allows prolonged underwater operations.

Upgrades are available, allowing the Type 209 to use the most advanced torpedoes and, in some cases, missiles.

Conversion to Air Independent Propulsion (AIP) requires the insertion of a new section of hull.

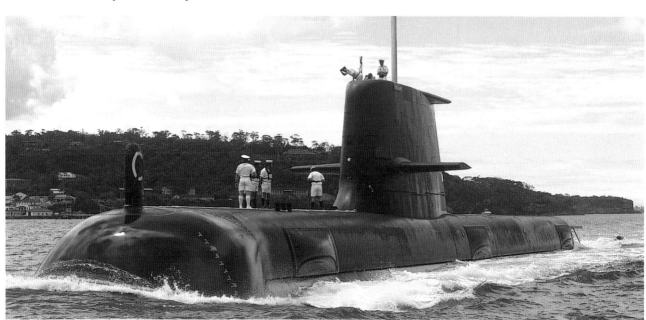

Type 206

Country	Germany
Launch Date	1973
Crew	23
Dimensions	48.6m x 4.6m x 4.5m (159ft 4in x 15ft 1in x 14ft 8in)
Displacement	
Surfaced	457 tonnes (450 tons)
Submerged	508 tonnes (500 tons)
Speed	
Submerged	17 knots
Surfaced	10 knots
Armament	8 × 533mm t-tubes, 8 DM2A1 Seeaal (206) or DM2A3 Seehecht, torpedoes; 24 mines
Powerplant	2 MTU 12V 493, four-stroke diesel engines, one Siemens-Schuckert- Werke electric motor
Range	Not known

Submarine and Anti-submarine Weapons

Some submarines can lay mines, and many can launch missiles. Ballistic missiles are strategic weapons and are of no real use in naval combat, but smaller missiles can be used to make 'standoff' attacks against surface ships and even land targets.

Most submarine-launched missiles are developed from conventional naval missiles, such as Sub-Harpoon, which is the submarine version of the successful Harpoon missile. It is also possible to launch long-range cruise missiles such as Tomahawk from a submarine's torpedo tubes. Anti-aircraft missile systems are not normally carried by submarines. Anti-aircraft armament was useful for boats that spent most of their time on the surface but today's submarines do not. However, there are submarine-launched anti-aircraft missile systems available. If fitted, they give a boat caught on the surface a chance to down a pursuing aircraft or helicopter and slip away before others arrive.

Torpedo Weights

Although missiles offer a range of impressive capabilities, the weapon of choice is still the torpedo. There are two basic types – heavy and light.

BELOW: Sub-Harpoon missiles can be launched through the torpedo tube, ejecting their protective capsule before reaching the air.

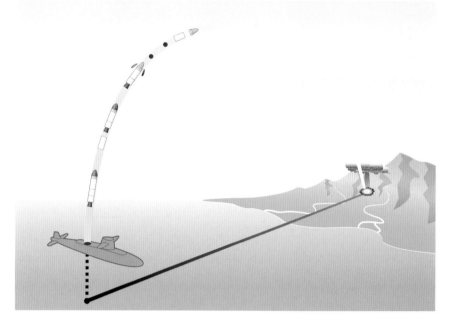

Lightweight torpedoes are often used as anti-submarine weapons, though they can attack vessels of all kinds. They are intended to attack by contact detonation, punching a hole in the enemy vessel's hull. Heavyweight torpedoes are intended to detonate under a surface ship. This creates a huge bubble of gas which lifts the middle of the vessel. The weight of the ends may then break the vessel's back. Even if this does not occur, the shock of a nearby underwater explosion can severely damage a ship.

Most modern torpedoes are either guided or capable of autonomously homing in on the target. Some have re-attack capability; that is, they can detect that they have missed and turn back for another pass. Torpedoes are also used to attack submarines. They may be dropped by aircraft, launched by CAPTOR

ABOVE: Submarine-launched ballistic missiles can attack land targets from a vast distance.

RIGHT: ASROC are 'standoff' anti-submarine weapons, delivering a homing torpedo to the target vicinity by rapid airborne flight.

(CAPtive TORpedo) mines, or fired from a vessel or another submarine. ASROC (AntiSubmarine ROCket) weapons deliver a torpedo into the water some distance from the launching vessel. It then homes in on the target.

Less sophisticated anti-submarine weapons are still in use. These include pattern-dropped explosives launched from an anti-submarine rocket launcher and depth charges. Nuclear torpedoes and depth charges are available but would not normally be used except amid an all-out major war.

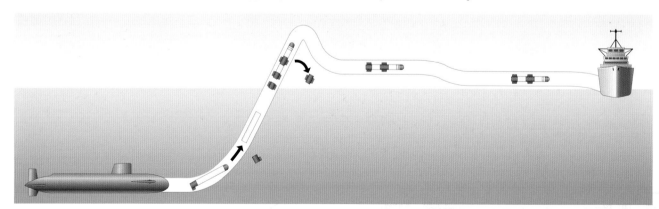

Propulsion, SONAR and Stealth

The submarine's worst

enemy is noise. Any sound it makes can be used to detect, locate and attack it. Similarly, all submarines carry sensitive instruments to listen for the noise of other vessels.

Ideally a target can be detected and located with passive measures only (without making any SONAR emissions that will give the sub's position away). If this is the case, the first indication that a sub is in the area may be the so-called 'flaming datum' – a burning and sinking ship. All submarines are designed to be as quiet as possible, with machinery mounted on rubber blocks to reduce vibration wherever possible. Hulls are often coated with anechoic (sound-absorbing) materials that both deaden the boat's own sounds and reduce the returns from enemy active SONAR.

Streamlined Silence

Another cause of noise is water turbulence caused by irregularities on the hull.

Vessels with a lot of openings and cavities produce a great deal of noise, especially at speed. Streamlined shapes and specially developed 'slippery' materials reduce this noise. Cavitation is a problem for a boat moving fast. Cavitation occurs when a boat's screw (or screws) cause air bubbles to be formed due to low pressure behind the blade. The deeper a boat is, the greater the water pressure and thus the faster its screw can rotate without cavitating. Submarines use a single, large, slowly-rotating screw in preference to multiple smaller screws for this reason – and also to reduce turbulence in the boat's wake. Overall, a boat that is moving slowly is much harder to detect than one that is travelling fast. A submarine moving at flank speed may make enough noise that it cannot detect other boats, and is effectively 'blind and deaf'.

SONAR

The uses of SONAR are not restricted to navigation and combat. Many submarines now mount mine-avoidance SONAR, which gives warning of nearby objects. This is unlikely to be of use if the boat is travelling at speed, but when moving more cautiously it can assist in sneaking

through a minefield or other obstructions. Ice-detection SONAR fulfils a similar purpose. SONAR systems can be mounted in various ways. The optimum position for gathering data for an attack is the bow of the boat, with passive systems along the flanks where they can pick up noise from all round the boat. Some submarines also use a towed SONAR array, which is trailed behind the boat. Each system has its own best position on the hull, depending on the job it is intended to do.

Yuri Dolgoruky

Country	Russia
Launch Date	February 2008
Crew	130
Displacement	
Surfaced	14,720 tonnes
	(14,488 tons)
Submerged	24,000 tonnes
	(23,621 tons)
Speed	
Surfaced	25 knots
Submerged	29 knots
Armament	16 × Bulava SLBMs,6 ×
	S-N-15 cruise missiles,
	533mm (21in) torpedo
	tubes
Powerplant	1 × OK-650B nuclear
	reactor, one AEU steam
	turbine, one shaft
Range	Unlimited except by
	food stores

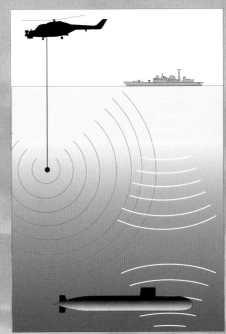

LEFT: Active SONAR systems can be mounted on vessels or dipped into the sea from a hovering helicopter. Using active SONAR gives away the emitter's position, so the decision to use it is a difficult one.

BELOW: *Yuri Dolgoruky*, lead ship of the Russian *Borei* class ballistic missile submarine, is designed to have a minimal noise signature and active SONAR return despite its size.

Civilian Submarines

Research and Commercial Usage

The possibility of an underwater transport remains attractive for various reasons. Submarines are not greatly affected by storms on the surface and can move under pack ice, making them useful on the northern sea route around Siberia and in similar icebound regions.

Safety Requirements

As yet, this is not a reality, but civilian submarines are involved in tourism as well as civilian research and commercial activities. One major concern in such areas is safety; navies will accept risks that civilian operators (and their insurers) will not. In the event that a submarine sinks in deep water there is little hope, as the boat will pass crush depth and be destroyed. However, if it hits the bottom before this, the crew may be rescued. The ideal method is to use a rescue vehicle which docks with the submarine's escape hatch and takes off the crew in safety.

Escape Systems

The Russian 'India' class submarines were designed to transport such rescue craft to the scene of an accident and then act as a receiving station for survivors. Other Deep Submergence Rescue Vehicles are air-transportable and can be on-station to conduct a rescue within hours. There are other ways to get out of crippled submarines. Obviously if diving suits are available, suitably trained personnel can use these to escape but the majority of submariners cannot do so. From the early years of the twentieth century, various escape apparatus has been in use.

Davis Escape Apparatus

Personal submarine escape systems began in 1910, with the Davis escape apparatus, which combined a rebreather unit to clean the air with a life jacket. Various similar systems have been used worldwide, and have been proven to work down to a depth of about 200m (656ft). Modern equipment like the US Submarine Escape Immersion Equipment (SEIE) includes thermal protection to prevent hypothermia in cold water and an inflatable life raft which can be used once the surface is reached.

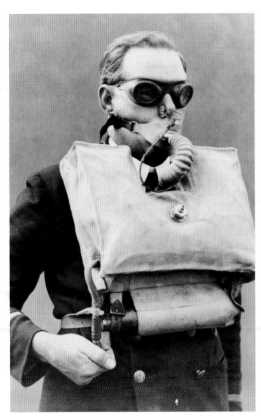

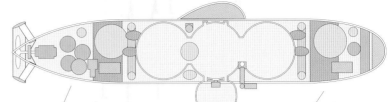

The vessel is operated by two crew, with two rescue personnel carried aboard and room for up to 24 other personnel.

The DRSV is designed to match the attitude of a submarine lying at an angle on the seabed.

ABOVE: The US Navy's *Mystic* class Deep Submergence Rescue Vehicle (DSRV) is carried to the rescue vicinity on a 'mother sub', then detaches to approach the distressed vessel.

LEFT: The Davis escape apparatus, allowed sunken submariners a chance of escape, but only in fairly shallow water.

BELOW: Submarine Escape Immersion Equipment (SEIE) suits allow escape from sunken vessels and act as a life raft on the surface.

Deep-ocean Exploration and Research

Until very recently, more was known about conditions on the Moon than in the deep oceans, and it seems that every time a mission is launched to the depths, several new species are discovered.

Mineral resources and new scientific discoveries about the way our world works are waiting to be found on the seabed – but getting down there can be a problem. The deep oceans are an alien world to humans. The enormous water pressure can crush a conventional submarine and diving equipment is useless as humans cannot survive at these depths. However, it has become possible to explore the ocean bottom trenches using a combination of crewed and remote-controlled submarines. These cannot make oceanic voyages under their own power – they are designed to go up and down, rather than traversing long distances – and are thus transported aboard surface vessels.

Discovering the Deep

Deep-diving submersibles started out with unpowered bathyspheres lowered from surface vessels and gradually developed into highly capable research submarines. Of necessity, these boats tend to be small and cramped, often using a spherical shape to help resist water pressure. Most have a fairing around the main equipment and operating chambers, to reduce drag and allow components to be attached to the outside of the boat. The discovery of hydrothermal vents in the seabed, creating a hot mineral-rich environment, generated new interest in deep-water exploration. The area around a vent is a unique ecosystem which can only be studied by using probes or manned submersibles. Research in this area led to the discovery of cold seeps,

a similar phenomenon which gives rise to a different set of ecological circumstances.

Living on the Seabed

In addition to enhancing biological and geological understanding, investigation of these deep-water phenomena is of benefit to industries that make extensive use of mineral resources, giving access to new sources of raw materials. Other underwater exploration projects are concerned with the behaviour of currents, seabed conditions and mineral deposits in areas that are not readily accessible, such as the mid-ocean seabed and areas under pack ice.

The Aquarius underwater laboratory project allows scientists to live on the seabed. Although it is located only 20m (66ft) down, it provides significant advantages in terms of the time that can be spent outside using diving gear. Transiting up and down to a support boat would greatly reduce the scientists' 'bottom time' and drive up costs. The Aquarius project has been running for some years and may lead to a more extensive underwater base in the future, perhaps located at greater depth.

ABOVE: Located off the Florida coast, Aquarius is an underwater laboratory where scientists live and work for extended periods.

RIGHT: The JIM suit allowed divers to work in water up to 400m (1300ft) deep without the need to decompress or breathe special gas mixes.

Wreck Location and Salvage

Salvage operations have been undertaken for as long as ships have existed, but up until the invention of the submarine, what could be achieved was strictly limited. Grabs lowered from surface vessels and divers swimming down to attach floats were the only real option.

Famous Wrecks

Since the submarine became available it has become possible to locate and explore wrecks in very deep water, and sometimes to salvage them or at least bring up some artefacts. Perhaps the most famous wrecks in the world – the liner *Titanic* and the battleship *Bismarck* – were both located by Robert Ballard and explored by manned and remote-controlled submarines. Many other vessels have been located and explored, in some cases solving long-standing mysteries about their fate or the reasons for their sinking.

Remote Reconnaissance

Operating in a deep-water wreck is a hazardous business. The wreck itself is rarely in a safe condition and usually has numerous protrusions or narrow openings. The danger is compounded by poor visibility. Salvage submarines carry powerful lights as there is no natural light in deep water, but the water is not always clear. The submarine itself may disturb debris, and there are always seabed currents to deal with. These can not only churn up the seabed, but may cause a submersible to drift into tangled wreckage. For this reason, remote-controlled probes equipped with cameras and lights are used to explore many wrecks.

The best-known submarine-related salvage operation was carried out by a surface vessel, the *Glomar Explorer*. This vessel was custom-designed to retrieve the wreck of a Soviet 'Golf'- class missile submarine from the ocean bed. The operation was a partial success. A cover story to maintain the secrecy of the operation suggested that *Glomar Explorer* was involved in seabed mining, attempting to retrieve manganese nodules from the seabed. This prompted interest in seabed mining. Exploration and prospecting operations are going on today, largely as a result of this invented story.

BELOW: The Phantom ROV (Remotely Operated Vehicle) enables wrecks to be investigated from the safety of a surface vessel.

The deep-submergence vessel *Aluminaut*, built for exploration in waters of up to 4500m (14,763ft) deep, was also involved in a novel salvage operation. In 1966, she assisted in the retrieval of a US Air Force nuclear bomb which had fallen from a B-52 bomber after a mid-air collision. Three years later *Aluminaut* recovered another deep-ocean submersible from the Atlantic seabed.

ABOVE: The search for the wreck of RMS *Titanic* caused great leaps forward in underwater exploration. The ship's wheel can be seen in this picture.

RIGHT: USS *Bluegill* was sunk and used as a salvage training site for 13 years. In 1984 she was raised and moved to deep water, ending 42 years of service to the US Navy.

Underwater Construction and Engineering Submarines

As the exploitation of deep waters continues to grow, submarines are increasingly necessary to assist in the construction and maintenance of structures and equipment. There is a limit to how deep divers can go and how long they stay down; a submarine allows longer-duration missions at greater depth. Submarines are used for survey work before a project begins and to support divers where appropriate. A detailed map of the seabed, water pressure and temperature conditions, salinity, currents and similar oceanographic data must be taken into consideration before a project can start. There is at present a fair amount of controversy over seabed mining and similar commercial operations, so it is likely that research will have to be undertaken into local ecological conditions before a project can proceed.

Survey and Safety

Once the project is actually begun, submarines permit a number of activities to be carried out with relative ease. Inspections of underwater pipelines and cables as well as the underwater components of oil-drilling rigs can be efficiently carried out by crewed or remotely-controlled vessels, and repairs can be made as necessary. Inspections of damage can also be made in the event that an accident occurs, increasing safety and reducing costs. Increasing use is being made of deep-diving robots for this kind of work. Known as ROVs (Remotely Operated Vehicles), these are essentially robotic submarines and do much the same work as a manned craft. At present remotely-controlled robotic vessels are standard, but there are hopes that in the near future fully autonomous craft can be introduced to handle routine work and thus free up assets for more complex tasks elsewhere.

Depth Advancement

The difficulties inherent in underwater engineering are similar to those that beset salvage and wreck location missions. Working in deep, dark water in close proximity to the legs of a drilling rig or the seabed can be hazardous

and requires considerable skill just to keep the submarine safe. If complex work must also be undertaken – often requiring very precise positioning of the craft – then the difficulty increases still further.

It is thought that there are vast mineral resources and large oilfields to be exploited on the seabed. Much of this wealth lies in very deep water.

The world's need for resources is set to continue increasing, so it is only logical that deep-water projects will become ever more important to the world economy, and that in turn will require ever more advanced vehicles to allow people to work in the depths of the seas.

Submarines continue to be an invaluable investment in the twenty-first century and development of these colossal vessels is ongoing.

TOP LEFT: Semi-submersible oil platforms can transit relatively shallow waters, taking on seawater as ballast to increase their draught.

TOP: The oil industry makes use of a range of remotely-operated vehicles for underwater work and inspection.

ABOVE: The Deep Rover submersible allows a single operator to undertake precision work in 1000m (3280ft) of water. It is designed to be no more difficult to operate than driving a car.

Index

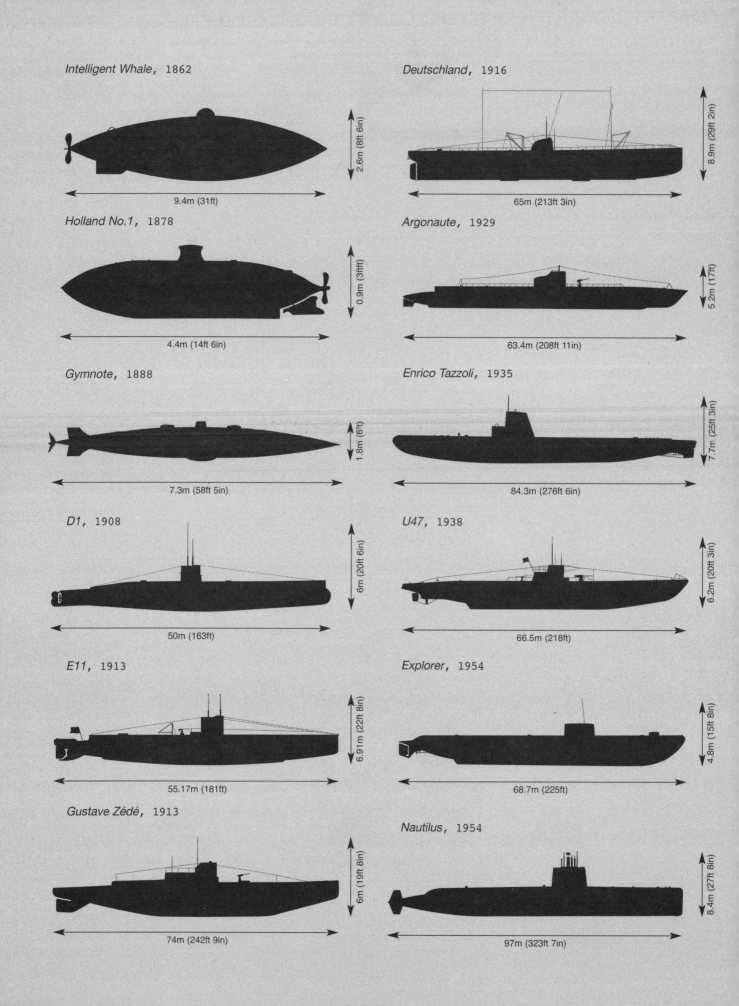

Intelligent Whale, 1862

2.6m (8ft 6in)

9.4m (31ft)

Holland No.1, 1878

0.9m (3ftft)

4.4m (14ft 6in)

Gymnote, 1888

1.8m (6ft)

7.3m (58ft 5in)

D1, 1908

6m (20ft 6in)

50m (163ft)

E11, 1913

6.91m (22ft 8in)

55.17m (181ft)

Gustave Zédé, 1913

6m (19ft 8in)

74m (242ft 9in)

Deutschland, 1916

8.9m (29ft 2in)

65m (213ft 3in)

Argonaute, 1929

5.2m (17ft)

63.4m (208ft 11in)

Enrico Tazzoli, 1935

7.7m (25ft 3in)

84.3m (276ft 6in)

U47, 1938

6.2m (20ft 3in)

66.5m (218ft)

Explorer, 1954

4.8m (15ft 8in)

68.7m (225ft)

Nautilus, 1954

8.4m (27ft 8in)

97m (323ft 7in)